I Always Wanted To Be Somebody

ALTHEA GIBSON

I Always Wanted To Be Somebody

ISBN: 978-1937559977

Re-Published in 2021

Originally published in 1960

Republished in 2021 by New Chapter Press
1175 York Ave., Suite #3S
New York, NY 10065
Randy Walker, Managing Partner
RWalker@NewChapterMedia.com
www.NewChapterMedia.com

TABLE OF CONTENTS

From The Publisher

When the Althea Gibson statue was dedicated at the U.S. Open in 2019, I remember hearing Billie Jean King say in a news interview how much of a hero and role model Gibson was to her as a young woman and how she used to go to bed at night with a copy of Gibson's book, *I Always Wanted To Be Somebody*, tucked under her pillow. I thought to myself, "I have to get a copy of that book and read it." However, when I went to Amazon.com to buy a copy of this book, originally published in 1960 , I saw that the only copy that was for sale was by a third-party vendor for $800. That was not right. Fans and young people need to have the opportunity to read Althea's story, in her own words, at a reasonable price. Althea Gibson is one of the most important and inspiring figures ever in the history of not just tennis, but global sport and society. I felt that I could perhaps be the one to try to correct this situation.

Since Fran Gray, the keeper of Althea's estate, had passed away shortly after the U.S. Open statue dedication, I was not sure who the right person was to speak with to revive and republish Althea's book. Via filmmaker Rex Miller, I was put in touch with Don Felder, Althea's second cousin. Along with Fran Gray's estate, I was able to work with them to bring *I've Always Wanted To Be Somebody* back into publication and make it available for sale to all at a reasonable price.

When reading the book, one should be reminded that it was written in the late 1950s and you may be surprised at some of the vocabulary and terminology, but this is how it was at the time, which also serves as an education of what a different era it was when Althea lived and competed. The book is republished how it was originally written and published by Althea back in the day. We felt it appropriate to have Billie Jean King add a Foreword to the book and we are thankful for her contribution and inspiration. We also want to also give a special thank you to Katrina Adams and Michelle Curry for their efforts in championing this effort.

We hope you enjoy *I Always Wanted To Be Somebody.*

—Randy Walker
New Chapter Press

FOREWORD

BILLIE JEAN KING

Althea Gibson was my shero and
she changed my life.

As an 11-year-old tennis was one of the most important things in my life. In those days there were not a ton of books about the sport, but I was able to find and read the few of them that were available at my local library. Those books, and that connection I made with tennis history were so important to me, I often slept with them.

At 11, after my first tennis instruction at a public park, I knew I wanted to be the number one player in the world. At 12, I was at the Los Angeles Tennis Club – then the mecca of tennis in Southern California – and I noticed everyone who played our sport wore white clothes and everyone who played was white. I asked myself, "Where is everyone else?" From that moment on I committed my life to a life of equality for everyone.

Tennis gave many of us a global platform and I knew if I could become the best player in the world, people might be more open to hearing what I had to say. But as a child I had no idea what it meant to be the best player in the world or what a "number one" looked like. At 13 I returned to the Los Angeles Tennis Club and there I got my answer. I saw Althea play for the very first time. Watching her play was almost like watching the ballet. Everything was perfect and she moved with grace, power and purpose. That was the day she became my shero.

I remember thinking to myself, "if that is what the best player in the world looks like, I have some work to do." But I knew, if you can see it, you can be it.

Her historic wins at the French Open in 1956 and Wimbledon in 1957 put her on the world's stage. Then in 1958 Althea released I Always Wanted to Be Somebody, and for the first time I got an insight into what she was thinking, what she was facing and what she was feeling. Her journey was not the typical tennis story, but it became one of the most important stories of my life and truly shaped my own journey, on and off the court.

By the early 1970s on the Virginia Slims Circuit we were starting to see the impact of Althea's presence when Bonnie Logan, Sylvia Hooks and Ann Koger became the first women of color on our new tour. Looking back, it was a historic moment, but like Althea, Bonnie, Sylvia and Ann never got the credit they deserved for being the trailblazers they were.

Over the years, I was very fortunate to get to know Althea and spend time with her. In 1968 we promoted "Tennis for Everyone" an exhibition tennis event in Oakland, California and it was important for me to include her and honor her for all she had done for our sport. Shortly before she passed Zina Garrison and I made a trip to see Althea and while it was hard to see her in failing health, it was still special to be in her presence.

Althea was our Jackie Robinson of tennis, and the barriers show broke down and the doors she opened have paved the way for generations of tennis players. Her contributions to our sport and to our world are many. Without Althea, there may not have been an Arthur Ashe, Leslie Allen, Zina Garrison, James Blake, Chanda Rubin, Mal Washington, Venus Williams, Serena Williams, Coco Gauff, Francis Tiafoe or Naomi Osaka.

If you can see it, you can be it.

1

WE WEREN'T BAD, JUST MISCHIEVOUS

I always wanted to be somebody. I guess that's why I kept running away from home when I was a kid even though I took some terrible whippings for it. It's why I took to tennis right away and kept working at it, even though I was the wildest tomboy you ever saw and my strong likings were a mile away from what the tennis people wanted me to do. It's why I've been willing to live like a gypsy all these years, always being a guest in other people's houses and doing things the way they said, even though what I've always craved is to live the way I want to in a place of my own with nobody to answer to but myself. It's why, ever since I was a wild, arrogant girl in my teens, playing stickball and basketball and baseball and paddle tennis and even football in the streets in the daytime and hanging around bowling alleys half the night, I've worshiped Sugar Ray Robinson. It wasn't just because he was a wonderful fellow, and good to me when there was no special reason for him to be; it was because he was somebody, an? I was determined that I was going to be somebody, too-if it killed me.

If I've made it, it's half because I was game to take a wicked amount of punishment along the way and half because there were an awful lot of people who cared, enough to help me. It has been a bewildering, challenging, exhausting experience, often more painful than pleasurable, more sad than happy. But I wouldn't have missed it for the world.

Not many people know the real story of my life before I got into the newspapers. I'm going to try to put it all down here, just the way I lived it and just the way I remember it. If you get to thinking it isn't all pretty, remember, I never said it was.

They tell me I was born on August 25, 1927, in a small town in South Carolina called Silver. I don't remember anything about Carolina; all I remember is New York. But my daddy talks about it a lot. He describes it as a three-store town, meaning that it wasn't as small as towns that only have one store for all the people. But it wasn't very big, either. My father, Daniel, and my mother, Annie, both lived in Silver. "I used to walk a mile over the bridge to see her once a week," he tells everybody. "Every Sunday night I went." And if you ask him how come he went to see Morn only once a week, he laughs and says, "Very simple. Cause that's all her people would allow it, that's why."

After they got married, my mother and father lived in a little cabin on a cotton farm. Daddy was helping one of my uncles sharecrop cotton and com, and there was plenty of hard work to go around. Daddy is a powerfully built man-he looks a lot like Roy Campanella, the famous Dodger catcher-and Mom is a strong woman; they had no trouble meeting the requirements. Mom is the first one to say that she was no delicate flower in those days. She used to love to ride, and because there wasn't much chance of her going to a riding stable, she used to ride not only horses but cows, hogs and everything. "Sure," she told me once, "I'd jump on that cow or that hog just like it was a horse. I believe I really could do some of that right now." I believe she could, too. She looks ten years younger than she is, and she's in shape. I was no weakling myself when I was born. I was the first child in the family, and I weighed a solid eight pounds. "You were what you call a big fat one," Mom says.

It's too bad I wasn't big enough to be of some help on the farm. They could have used me. Daddy and my uncle only had five acres of land and they never had a chance of making out. Even if things had gone well, they couldn't have put anything by. But when bad weather ruined the crops three years in a row, they were in bad shape. "I worked three years for nothin,'" Daddy says. "That third year, all I got out of it was a bale and a half of cotton. Cotton was sellin' for fifty dollars a bale then, so I made seventy-five dollars for the year's work. I had to get out of there, and when Mom's sister, Sally Washington, came down from New York for their sister Blanche's funeral, I made up my mind it was time."

What Daddy did was agree to let Aunt Sally take me back to New York with her on the understanding that he would come up a couple of months later and get a job, and then, as soon as he could, send for Mom. He came as soon as he got the cash for his bale and a half of cotton. "I bought me a cheap blue suit for seven dollars and fifty cents," he says, "I paid twenty-five dollars for the fare, I left some money with the wife, and I took off for New York City."

I never get tired of hearing Daddy tell about what happened to him when he got off the train in New York. He had been talking to this porter on the train, telling him how bad things had been in South Carolina, and when the train pulled into Pennsylvania Station he asked the porter how to get to Harlem. The porter said it was pretty hard even for somebody who knew his way around the city, but that he could spare an hour to guide him if Daddy wanted to pay him five dollars for his time and trouble. Daddy agreed, and the porter took him over to the subway and got on with him. After about twenty minutes, he led him out on the sidewalk at 125th Street and said, "Here you are, Mr. Gibson. This is Harlem." And so Daddy started his life in the big city by paying five dollars for a nickel ride on the subway.

"But that was all right," I remember Daddy saying at a party once. "It didn't make no difference. I got me a job right away, handyman in a garage, for big money. Ten dollars a week. I didn't have nothin' to worry about no more. I sent for my wife and we were in business."

We all lived together in Aunt Sally's apartment for quite a while before Daddy and Mom got an apartment of their own. I was only three years old when Aunt Sally first brought me up with her, and I don't remember very much about what it was like at her place. I do know she made good money selling bootleg whisky; I don't think she actually made the stuff, I think she just sold it. Whether or not she had any other source of income, I don't know, but if she did, it was closely mixed up with selling the whisky to the men who were always coming to the house. I know one thing. There was always lots of food to eat in her house, the rent was always paid on time, and Aunt Sally wore nice clothes every day in the week. She did all right for herself.

There was one time when her business was bad for me. I was in my bedroom, sleeping, and Aunt Sally was in the parlor with her company. I woke up feeling awful thirsty and I got up to get a glass of water in the kitchen. I noticed a big jug on the kitchen table, and it looked good, so without even thinking twice, I grabbed it and turned it up. The next thing I can remember is Aunt Sally holding me down in the bed while the doctor pumped my stomach out.

According to Daddy, that was far from the last time in my kid days that I put away a lot of whisky. Some of my uncles, and some of the other men who came to see Aunt Sally, used to take me out with them for the afternoon, and naturally they would always end up drinking whisky. So would I. They gave it to me in a water glass, and without any water in it, either. Daddy claims that I never used to get drunk but that when I got home he had to get all the whisky out of me. I don't ask him any more how he managed to do it but I have a better than vague recollection that it had something to do with sticking two of his fingers down my throat. I don't recommend this kind of childhood training, but I will say one thing for it-I don't think I'll ever disgrace myself by getting drunk in public. I've built up a sort of immunity.

When I was about seven or eight, I went to Philadelphia to live for a while with my aunt Daisy Kelly, who lives in the Bronx now, in New York City. I stayed with Aunt Daisy off and on for a couple of years, and I must have given her plenty of trouble, although now she just makes it all sound kind of comical. I've heard her tell one story a hundred times, and no matter how funny it sounds now, it must have been a sore trial at the time. Aunt Daisy had this friend who owned a secondhand automobile, and I admired the car and him very much. I used to follow him around everywhere. "This particular morning," Aunt Daisy says, "it was Sunday, and I'd got you all dressed up in a beautiful white dress, with white stockings and even a white silk bow in your hair. Then I let you go out. You were gone a long time, and after a while I began to get worried, so I started looking out the window for you. And there that man was working on his car, and he had an open bucket of grease standing on the sidewalk next to it, and you were jumping across the bucket, first from one side and then from the other. And sure enough, just when I was sucking in air to scream at you, you slipped and fell right in the damn bucket. You looked like Amos and Andy. I couldn't get the last of that grease off you for days, and the dress--I just had to throw the dress away."

Another day, Aunt Daisy says, when I was gone long, I finally came around the corner with a great big branch of a tree in my hand, and two boys running after me as hard as they could run. According to Aunt Daisy, just when it looked like they were going to catch up to me and really give it to me, I turned around and started swinging that branch on them. "You just frailed them and frailed them," she says. "I started out being scared that you were going to get hurt, and I wound up being scared that you would hurt them bad." I could always take care of myself pretty well, that's a fact.

I think the worst fright I ever gave Aunt Daisy was once when she and my cousin Pearl were going somewhere in a friend's car, and I wasn't supposed to go. I kicked up a storm and then quietly made up my mind what I was going to do. When the car pulled up at the house they were going to, and Aunt Daisy and Pearl got out, I was standing on the sidewalk. I had made the whole trip standing on the running board and holding on to the door handle, with my head scrooched down underneath the window so nobody could see me.

But I didn't start getting into real trouble until the Gibson family settled into a place of its own, the apartment on West 143rd Street in which my mother and father, my sisters, Millie and Annie and Lillian, and my brother Daniel, still live. I was a traveling girl, and I hated to go to school. What's more, I didn't like people telling me what to do. Take it from me, you can get in a lot of hot water thinking like that.

I played hooky from school all the time. It was a habit I never lost. Later on, when I got bigger, my friends and I used to regard school as just a good place to meet and make our plans for what we would do all day. When I was littler, the teachers used to try to change me; sometimes they would even spank me right in the classroom. But it didn't make any difference, I'd play hooky again the next day. Daddy would whip me, too, and I'm not talking about spankings. He would whip me good, with a strap on my bare skin, and there was nothing funny about it. Sometimes I would be scared to go home and I would go to the police station on 135th Street and tell them that I was afraid to go home because my father was going to beat me up. The first time I did it, the cops let me stay there for about an hour and then they called Mom and told her to come and get me. But she was afraid to go. She didn't want any part of police stations. So, finally, the desk sergeant sent a young cop over to the house to ask her, "Don't you want your daughter?" I got it good that night.

The only thing I really liked to do was play ball. Basketball was my favorite, but any kind of ball would do. I guess the main reason why I hated to go to school was because I couldn't see any point in wasting all that time that I could be spending shooting baskets in the playground. "She was always the outdoor type," Daddy told a reporter once. "That's why she can beat that tennis ball like nobody's business." If I had gone to school once in a while like I was supposed to, Daddy wouldn't have minded my being a tomboy at all. In fact, I'm convinced that he was disappointed when I was born that I wasn't a boy. He wanted a son. So he always treated me like one, right from when I was a little tot in Carolina and we used to shoot marbles in the dirt road with acorns for marbles. He claims I used to beat him all the time but seeing that I was only three years old then, I think he's exaggerating a little bit. One thing he isn't exaggerating about, though, is when he says he wanted me to be a prize fighter. He really did. It was when I was in junior high school, like maybe twelve or thirteen years old, and he'd been reading a lot about professional bouts between women boxers, sort of like the women's wrestling they have in some parts of the country today. (Women's boxing is illegal now but in those days it used to draw some pretty good small-club gates.) Daddy wanted to put me in for it. "It would have been big," he says. "You would have been the champion of the world. You were big and strong, and you could hit."

I know it sounds indelicate, corning from a girl, but I could fight, too. Daddy taught me the moves, and I had the right temperament for it. I was tough, I wasn't afraid of anybody, not even him. He says himself that when he would whip me, I would never cry, not if it killed me. I would just sit there and look at him. I wouldn't sass him back or anything, but neither would I give him the satisfaction of crying. He would be doing all the hitting and all the talking, and I guess after a while it must have seemed like a terrible waste of time. He liked our boxing lessons better. He would say, "Put up your dukes," and I had to get ready to defend myself or I would take an even worse beating. He would box with me for an hour at a time, showing me how to punch, how to jab, how to block punches, and how to use footwork. He did a good job on me, maybe too good. I remember one day he got mad at me for not coming home for a couple of nights, and he didn't waste any time going for the strap. When I finally sashayed in, he just walked up to me and punched me right in the face and knocked me sprawling down the hall. I got right back up and punched him as hard as I could, right in the jaw, and we had a pretty good little fight going and we weren't fooling around, either. Daddy weighs about one hundred and ninety pounds. He's fond of saying, "I can take any one man. Maybe a gang could take care of me, but one man, that's, out of the question. If I give him one punch, he ain't going to bother me anymore." But I took a shot at him just the same.

Of course, once he got the idea of me boxing professionally out of his head, all Daddy was trying to do, aside from teach me right from wrong, was to make sure I would be able to protect myself. Harlem is a mean place to grow up in; there's always somebody to gall you no matter how much you want to mind your own business. If Daddy hadn't shown me how to look out for myself, I would have got into a lot of fights that I would have lost, and I would have been pretty badly beaten up a lot of times. I remember once I was walking down the street with a bunch of pebbles in my hand, throwing them at targets like street signs and mailboxes and garbage cans, and this big girl came up to me and said, "What, are you supposed to be tough or something? You're supposed to be bad?" I tried to pay no mind to her. I wanted to avoid her. But she wouldn't let me. She hauled off and hit me right in the breadbasket and I went down to my knees, in agony. I prayed that she wouldn't hit me again while I was trying to get my breath back. But she didn't; she just walked away, and I ran home crying. Daddy didn't give me any sympathy at all. When I told him what had happened, he said, "If you don't go back out there and find her and whip her, I'll whip the behind off you when you come home." So I went back and I found her and I beat the hell out of her. I really tore into her. I kept hitting and hitting, and I wasn't hitting like a girl, either, I was punching. Every time I hit her in the belly and she doubled up with the pain, I straightened her up again with a punch in the face. I didn't show her any mercy, but I guarantee you one thing, she never bothered me again.

Sometimes, in a tough neighborhood, where there is no way for a kid to prove himself except by playing games and fighting, you've got to establish a record for being able to look out for yourself before they will leave you alone. If they think you're an easy mark, they will all look to build up their own reputations by beating up on you. I learned always to get in the first punch. There was one fight I had with a big girl who sat in back of me in school. Maybe because I wasn't there very often, she made life miserable for me when I did show up. I used to wear my hair long, in pigtails, then, and she would yank on those pigtails until I thought she was going to tear my hair out by the roots. If I turned around and asked her to leave me alone, she would just pull harder the next time. So one day I told her I'd had all of that stuff I was going to take, and I'd meet her outside after school and we would see just how bad she was. The word that there was going to be a fight spread all around the school, and by the time I walked outside that afternoon, she was standing in the playground waiting for me, and half the school was standing behind her ready to see the fun. I was scared. I wished I hadn't started the whole thing. She was a lot bigger than me, and she had the reputation of being a tough fighter. But I didn't have any choice. I had to save my face the best way I could. Anyway, my whole gang was behind me, pushing me right up to her.

We stood there for a minute or so, our faces shoved up against each other, the way kids will do, and we cursed each other and said what we were going to do to each other. Meanwhile I tried to get myself into position, so I'd have enough leverage to get off a good punch. She had just got through calling me a pig-tailed bitch when I let her have it. I brought my right hand all the way up from the floor and smashed her right in the face with all my might. I hit her so hard she just fell like a lump. Honest to God, she was out cold. Everybody backed away from me and just stared at me, and I turned around like I was Joe Louis and walked on home.

It wasn't only girls that I fought, either. I had one terrible fight with a boy, on account of my

Uncle Junie, who was Aunt Sally Washington's brother, Charlie. They were living on 144th Street, just off Edgecombe, and there was a tough gang on the block called the Sabres. The leader of the gang and I used to pal around together a lot; we played stickball and basketball and everything. No loving up, though. I wasn't his girl. We were what we called boon-coons, which in Harlem means block buddies, good friends. Well, this one day I'd been up visiting Aunt Sally, and on my way out, just as I turned around the last landing, I saw Uncle Junie lolling on the stairs, slightly intoxicated, and this Sabre leader was standing over him going through his pockets. What you doin'?" I hollered down at him. "That's my uncle! Go bother somebody else if you got to steal, but don't bother him!" I ran down and -lifted Uncle Junie up, got him turned around, and started to help him up the stairs. Then I looked back over my shoulder to see if the kid was leaving, and I was just in time to see him take a sharpened screwdriver out of his pocket and throw it at me. I stuck my hand out to protect myself and got a gash just above my thumb that still shows a scar as plain as day. Well, I got Uncle Junie upstairs as quick as I could and went back down after that boy and we had a fight that they still talk about on 144th Street. We fought all over the block, and first he was down and then I was down, but neither of us would stay down if we died for it. He didn't even think of me as a girl, I can assure you. He fought me with his fists and his elbows and his knees and even his teeth. We were both pretty bloody and bruised when some big people finally stopped it, and I guess you would have to say it was a draw. But at least those Sabres respected me from then on. None of them ever tried to use me for a dartboard again.

Once I took a punch at Uncle Junie himself. I walked into his apartment one night when he was having a big fight with his wife, Mabel. Just as I came in, Uncle Junie hauled off and slapped Mabel as hard as he could, right across her face. Well, that was all I had to see. I was little lady Robin Hood in the flesh. I sashayed right up to him and punched him in the jaw as hard as I could and knocked him down on his back. "What the hell are you hittin' Mabel like that for?" I hollered at him. I was lucky he didn't get up and knock all my teeth out.

Except for the fights I got into, and playing hooky all the time, I didn't get into much serious trouble when I was a kid or do anything very bad. I guess about the worst thing we did was snitch little packages of ice cream while we were walking through the big stores like the five-and-ten, or pieces of fruit while we were walking past a stand on the street. I remember once a gang of us decided we would snitch some yams for roasting, and I strolled nonchalantly past the stand and casually lifted one. Once I had it, though, I couldn't resist the impulse to run, and a cop who was standing on the corner got curious and grabbed me, for good luck. He had me cold; I had that damn yam right in my hand. I'd have run if I could, but he had a death grip on my arm and he dragged me over to the police call box and made like he was going to call up for the wagon to come and get me. I was scared. I begged him to let me go. I swore I'd be a good girl for the whole rest of my life. Finally, he said he would give me a break, and he took me over to the stand and made me put back the yam, and then he let me go. But when I walked around the comer and found the rest of the girls I'd been with, they dared me to go back and get it again, and I was just bold enough to take the dare. I got it, too, and got away clean, and we went and built a fire on an empty lot in the next block and roasted it.

Sometimes we used to go across the 145th Street Bridge to the Bronx Terminal Market, where all the freight cars full of fruits and vegetables are broken down for the wholesalers. That was a snitcher's heaven. They used to stack rejects off to one side, stuff that the wholesalers wouldn't accept, and we'd sneak in with empty baskets and try to fill them up before they spotted us and came after us. Sometimes I'd get a whole basketful of overripe bananas and peaches, wilted lettuce and soft tomatoes, and we'd really gorge ourselves on the stuff. Once I carried a whole watermelon in my hands over that bridge.

Like I said, we never got in any real trouble. We were just mischievous. I think one good thing was that I never joined any of those so-called social clubs that they've always had in Harlem. None of my girl friends did, either. We didn't care for that stuff, all the drinking and narcotics and sex that they went in for in those clubs-and we didn't care for the stickups that they turned to sooner or later in order to get money for the things they were doing. I didn't like to go to school but I had no interest in going to jail, either. Mostly my best girl friend, Alma Irving, and I liked to play hooky and spend the day in the movies, especially on Friday, when they had a big stage show at the Apollo Theatre on 125th Street. Alma liked to play basketball, too, almost as much as I did. She was a good basket shooter, and we'd spend hours in the park shooting for Cokes or hot dogs. At night we used to go to the school gymnasium and challenge anybody, boy or girl, man or woman, to play us in what we used to call two-on-two. We'd use just one basket and see which team could score the most baskets on the other. We played hard, and when we got finished, we'd go to a cheap restaurant and get a plate of collard greens and rice, or maybe, if we were a little flush, a hamburger steak or fried chicken and French fried potatoes. In those days, of course, you could get a big plate of food like that for only thirty-five cents. Fish and chips were only fifteen cents, and soda was a nickel a quart if you brought your own can. You could buy big sweet potatoes-we called them mickeys-for a couple of cents apiece, and they tasted awful good roasted over an open fire made out of broken-up fruit crates that we picked up in the alleyway behind the A&P. Now I realize how poor we were in those days, and how little we had. But it didn't seem so bad then. How could you feel sorry for yourself when soda was a nickel a quart?

We had some great adventures. I had a friend, Charles, who was twelve years old and, like me, was always ready to go. One time we made up our minds to go to the World's Fair out on Long Island. We got together some change by scrounging all the empty soda bottles we could find and turning them in at the store; we got two cents for Coke bottles and ginger ale and soda splits, and a nickel apiece for the big quart bottles. Then we went to the bicycle store and rented a bike for the day for thirty five cents, and we rode all the way out to the World's Fair in Flushing Meadows, taking turns with one of us driving and the other one sitting on the bar. When we got there, we walked around until we spotted a place where we could sneak in, and we had a big time all afternoon and then pedaled all the way back home to Harlem.

Another time, Charles and I rented a bike up around 145th Street, rode it down to another bicycle store a couple of blocks below 125th Street, and sold it for three dollars so we could go to Coney Island. We didn't get back home until midnight, and in the meantime the man we had rented the bike from had come to the house looking for it. We'd had to give him our names and addresses when we took it out. Looking back on it, I have no idea how we thought we were going to get away with it. I guess we had some notion that maybe the man who owned the bike wouldn't look for it for a couple of days, and in the meantime we could make a few bucks somewhere and buy it back from the man we'd sold it to. What happened was that the next morning Daddy took me downtown and gave the man his three dollars and got the bike back. The man didn't want to let us have it at first, but when Daddy explained that we'd stolen it, he gave it up in a hurry. He didn't want to have any trouble with the police. I had a sore bottom for a week after that little business deal, and it wasn't from riding the handlebars, either.

Poor Daddy must have wished there was some way he could whip me hard enough to make me behave like the other kids in the family. My brother Dan and my three sisters, Millie and Annie and Lillian, never got into any trouble at all. They were good in school, too. I was the only one who was always stepping out of line.

I think my worst troubles started when I graduated from junior high school in 1941. How I ever managed to graduate, I don't know, but I guess I was there just often enough to find out a little bit about what was going on. Either that or they simply made up their minds to pass me on to the next school and let them worry about me. It might have worked except that I didn't like the idea of going to the Yorkville Trade School, which was where I'd been transferred to. It wasn't that I really cared which school I went to or played hooky from; it was just that a lot of my girl friends were going to one of the downtown high schools, and I wanted to stay with them. I tried to get changed over, but they wouldn't let me, and that didn't set well with me at all.

I guess I went pretty regularly for the first year, mostly because I was interested in the sewing classes. I got to be pretty good on the sewing machine. I remember once something went wrong with the machine I was using, and I volunteered to fix it, and I did. The teacher was amazed. But after a while I got tired of the whole thing, and from then on school and I had nothing in common at all. I began to stay out for weeks at a time, and because the truant officer would come looking for me, and then Daddy would whip me, I took to staying away from home, too. Mom says she used to walk the streets of Harlem until two or three o'clock in the morning looking for me. But she never had much chance of finding me. When I was really trying to hide out I never went near any of the playgrounds or gymnasiums or restaurants that I usually hung out at. I sneaked around to different friends' houses in the daytime, or sat all by myself in the movies, and then, if I didn't have any place lined up to sleep, I would just ride the subway all night. I would ride from one end of the line to the other, from Van Cortlandt Park to New Lots Avenue, back and forth like a zombie. At least it was a place to sit down.

Naturally, the longer I would stay away the worse beating I would get when I finally did go home. So I would just stay away longer the next time. It got so that my mother was afraid to let me out of the house for fear I wouldn't come back. Sooner or later, though, she would take a chance and give me fifteen or twenty cents and send me down to the store for a loaf of bread or a bottle of milk. I would go downstairs and see the boys playing stickball in the street, and that would be the last I thought of the loaf of bread or the bottle of milk. I would play until it got dark, spend the money on something to eat, and take off on another lonesome expedition.

Once a girl friend of mine whose parents had been really cruel to her, so bad that she'd had to go to the police about it, told me there was a place on Fifth Avenue at 105th Street called the Society for the Prevention of Cruelty to Children, that would take in kids who were in trouble and had no place to go.

The next time I stayed out so late that I didn't dare go home I remembered about this place and went there and asked them to take me in. 'Tm scared to go home," I told the lady in charge. "My father will whip me something awful." They took me in and gave me a bed to sleep in, in a big girls' dormitory, and it was a whole lot better than riding the subway. The beds had white sheets and everything. The trouble was, they notified my mother and father that they had me there, and Daddy came for me in the morning and took me home. I promised him I wasn't ever going to run away again, but he licked me anyway, and a week later I took off again. I went straight to the S.P.C.C. I told them that my father had whipped me bad, after he'd promised that he wouldn't, and I even skinned off my shirt and showed them the big red welts the strap ad put on my back. They took me in again, and this time when Daddy came after me they asked me if I wanted to go back with him. When I said no, that I was afraid to, they said I could stay if I wanted to. I wanted to, all right. As far as I was concerned, that place was a regular country club. I had to do a little work, like making my bed and helping clean up the dormitory, and taking my tum scrubbing the toilets, but mostly it was a snap. At home I'd had to work a lot harder, the food was nowhere near as good, and somebody was always yelling at me or, worse, hitting me. This was my idea of living.

The only time it was bad was when I got into a fight with one of the other girls and they punished me by putting me down in the solitary cell, which wasn't really a cell at all but just a little room in the basement where all you had was a mattress on the bare floor and nothing very much to eat. I behaved myself after that experience; I didn't want to go back there again. It was too nice up in the dorm.

After a while, though, I got tired of the life there. I guess it was a little too restricted for me. So I told the head lady I wanted to go back home, and she said, all right, I could, but that if I had any more trouble they would have to send me away to the girls' correction school, which is polite language for reformatory, at Hudson, in upstate New York. They sent for Daddy and released me in his custody. I was a little nervous about what he might do, but I was glad to be going home anyway.

I want to say right here that none of this is meant to say that my father was harder on me than he ought to have been. Even though when he got mad he got very mad, he was actually a patient man. If he had whipped me every day of my life from the time I was seven years old, I would have deserved it. I gave him a whole lot of trouble. I don't hate him for anything today. In fact, I love him. I feel a lot of those whippings he gave me helped make me what I am today. Somebody had to knock a little sense into me, and it wasn't easy.

I had no intention of going back to that Yorkville Trade School, but I was too young to get my working papers, so I had to make a deal with the school people. They let me have working papers on condition that I would go to night school a certain number of hours a week. I went for a couple of weeks, but then I stopped, and nobody ever came after me. So that was that. I was officially a working girl. I liked it, too. I felt better, working. I had the feeling of being independent, like I was somebody, making my own money and buying what I wanted to buy, paying in a little at home and doing what I wanted to do instead of being what you might call dictated to. It was very important to me to be on my own.

I must have worked at a dozen jobs in the next few years, maybe more. I was restless and I never stayed in any one place very long. If it wasn't to my liking, I quit. I was a counter girl at the Chambers Street branch of the Chock Full O' Nuts restaurant chain. I was a messenger for a blueprinting company. I worked in a button factory and a dress factory and a department store. I ran an elevator in the Dixie Hotel, and I even had a job cleaning chickens in a butcher shop. I used to have to take out the guts and everything, but I still like to eat chicken. Out of all of them, I only had one job that I really liked, and I lost that one for being honest. It was at the New York School of Social Work. I was the mail clerk, and I even had a little office of my own. It was my job to sort all the mail for the whole school, break it down and deliver it to the different offices and people, and also take care of sending out the outgoing mail. I liked the job because it was the first one I'd had that gave me some stature, that made me feel like I was somebody. I was there for six months, the longest I ever worked at any job. I lost it because one Friday some of my girl friends were taking the day off to go to the Paramount Theatre in Times Square to see Sarah Vaughan in the stage show, and I decided I would go, too.

When I went in to work on Monday morning, the lady supervisor sent for me to come into her office, and I knew right away I was in trouble. "What happened to you on Friday?" she wanted to know. I could have lied to her and told her I'd been sick, but I didn't feel like it. I told her the truth. "All my girl friends were going to the Paramount to see the show," I told her. "Sarah Vaughan was there. I thought maybe it wouldn't be so bad if I took just one day off. I'm sorry about it. I won't do it again, I promise." For a minute, I thought she was going to let me off. "I must say I admire your honesty," she said. "I would much rather you told me the truth than have you lie to me. But that doesn't change the fact that your job here is particularly important to the whole organization. We've got have an especially trustworthy person in it. I had to do all the mail by myself on Friday, and it was late getting around. I simply can't have somebody in that job who would leave it untended for such a foolish reason. I'll have to let you go and get somebody else."

The kind of girl I was at the time, it wasn't easy for me to beg anybody for anything. But I really begged that lady to let me stay. "I'll never do it again," I told her, "honest I won't. I'll come to work even if I'm sick." But she wouldn't change her mind. "The only thing I can do for you," she said, "is give you a week's pay to give you a chance to find another job. But you're through here. You'll have to leave today."

It wasn't exactly the best way for me to learn that it pays to be honest, but it was a good way for me to learn that it pays to stick to your responsibilities. I sure liked that job. I hated to lose it.

For a while I didn't exactly knock myself out looking for another job. I suppose you could say I was sulking. Anyway, I just stayed away from home and bummed around the streets. It wasn't long before a couple of women from the Welfare Department picked me up and laid down the law. If I wouldn't live home, and I wouldn't go to school, I would have to let them find me a place to stay with a good, respectable family and report to them every week so they could keep a check on me. Either that or I would have to go away to the reformatory; one or the other. Naturally, when they put it like that, I said I would go along with what they wanted. So they got me a furnished room in a private home, and even gave me an allowance to live off while I was looking for a job. I could hardly believe this allowance jazz. It was too good to be true. But I figured I might as well enjoy it while I could, so I forgot all about looking for a job and just spent all my time playing in the streets and the parks and going to the movies. I went back to see my mother and father fairly often, and they made no objection to what I was doing because they figured I was in good hands with the Welfare ladies. I sure was never better. All I had to do was report in once a week and pick up my allowance. It was during this time, when I was living in a never-never land through the courtesy of the City of New York, that I was introduced to tennis. My whole life was changed, just like that, and I never even knew it was happening.

2

BETWEEN TWO WORLDS

The 143rd Street block my mother and father lived on was a Police Athletic League play street, which means that the policemen put up wooden barricades at the ends of the street during the daytime and closed it to traffic so we could use it for a playground. One of the big games on the street was paddle tennis, and I was the champion of the block. In fact, I even won some medals representing 143rd Street in competition with other Harlem play streets. I still have them, too. I guess I've kept every medal or trophy I ever won anywhere.

Paddle tennis is played on a court marked off much like a tennis court, only about half the size. You use a wooden racket instead of a gut racket, and you can play with either a sponge rubber ball or a regular tennis ball. It's a lot different from real tennis, and yet it's a lot like it, too. There was a musician fellow, Buddy Walker, who's known now as "Harlem's Society Orchestra Leader," but who in those days didn't get much work in the summer months and filled in by working for the city as a play leader. He was watching me play paddle tennis one day when he suddenly got the idea that I might be able to play regular tennis just as well if I got the chance. So, out of the kindness of his heart, he bought me a couple of second-hand tennis rackets for five dollars apiece and started me out hitting balls against the wall on the handball courts at Morris Park. Buddy got very excited about how well I hit the ball, and he started telling me all about how much I would like the game and how it would be a good thing for me to become interested in it because I would meet a better class of people and have a chance to make something out of myself. He took me up to his apartment to meet his wife, Trini, and their daughter, Fern, and we all talked about it.

The next thing that happened was that Buddy took me to the Harlem River Tennis Courts at 150th Street and Seventh Avenue and had me play a couple of sets with one of his friends. He always has insisted that the way I played that day was phenomenal for a young girl with no experience, and I remember that a lot of the other players on the courts stopped their games to watch me. It was very exciting; it was a competitive sport and I am a competitive sort of person. When one of the men who saw me play that first time, a Negro schoolteacher, Juan Serrell, suggested to Buddy that he would like to try to work out some way for me to play at the Cosmopolitan Tennis Club, which he belonged to, I was more than willing. The Cosmopolitan is gone now, but in those days, it was the ritzy tennis club in Harlem. All the Sugar Hill society people belonged to it.

Mr. Serrell's idea was to introduce me to the members of the Cosmopolitan and have me play a few sets with the club's one-armed professional, Fred Johnson, so that everybody could see what I could do. If I looked good enough, maybe some of them would be willing to chip in to pay for a junior membership for me and to underwrite the cost of my taking lessons from Mr. Johnson. Lucky for me, that's the way it worked out. Everybody thought I looked like a, real good prospect, and they took up a collection and I bought me a membership. I got a regular schedule of lessons from Mr. Johnson, and I began to learn something about the game of tennis. I already knew how to hit the ball but I didn't know why. He taught me some footwork and some court strategy, and along with that he also tried to help me improve my personal ways. He didn't like my arrogant attitude and he tried to show me why I should change. I don't think he got too far in that department; my mind was set pretty strong. I was willing to do what he said about tennis, but I figured what I did away from the courts was none of his business. I wasn't exactly ready to start studying how to be a fine lady.

Those days, I probably would have been more at home training in Stillman's Gym than at the Cosmopolitan Club. I really wasn't the tennis type. But the polite manners of the game, that seemed so silly to me at first, gradually began to appeal to me. So did the pretty white clothes. I had trouble as a competitor because I kept wanting to fight the other player every time, I started to lose a match. But I could see that certain things were expected, in fact required, in the way of behavior on a tennis court, and I made up my mind that I would go along with the program. After a while I began to understand that you could walk out on the court like a lady, all dressed up in immaculate white, be polite to everybody, and still play like a tiger and beat the liver and lights out of the ball. I remember thinking to myself that it was kind of like a matador going into the bull ring, beautifully dressed, bowing in all directions, following the fancy rules to the letter, and all the time having nothing in mind except sticking that sword into the bull's guts and killing him as dead as hell. I probably picked up that notion from some movie I saw.

I suppose if Fred Johnson or the club members who were paying for my tennis had known the whole truth about the way I was living I wouldn't have lasted long. The Cosmopolitan members were the highest class of Harlem people and they had rigid ideas about what was socially acceptable behavior. They were undoubtedly more strict than white people of similar position, for the obvious reason that they felt they had to be doubly careful in order to overcome the prejudiced attitude that all Negroes lived eight to a room in dirty houses and drank gin all day and settled all their arguments with knives. I'm ashamed to say I was still living pretty wild. I was supposed to be looking for a job, but I didn't look very hard because I was too busy playing tennis in the daytime and having fun at night. The hardest work I did, aside from practicing tennis, was to report to the Welfare ladies once a week, tell them how I was getting along, and pick up my allowance. Then I would celebrate by spending the whole day in the movies and filling myself up with a lot of cheap food. But I guess it would have been too much to expect me to change completely right away. Actually, I realize now that every day I played tennis and got more interested in the game, I was changing a little bit. I just wasn't aware of it.

One of the people who did a lot for me in those early days at the Cosmopolitan was Mrs. Rhoda Smith. She has been important to me ever since. Rhoda is a well-off society woman who had lost her own daughter about ten years before I met her, and she practically adopted me. She bought me my first tennis costume and did everything she could to give me a boost. I didn't always appreciate it, either, and I guess Rhoda was well aware of it. I clipped a newspaper story a few years ago in which she told a reporter: "I was the first woman Althea ever played tennis with, and she resented it because I was always trying to improve her ways. I kept saying, 'Don't do this,' and 'Don't do that,' and sooner or later she would holler, 'Mrs. Smith, you're always pickin' on me.' I guess I was, too, but I had to. When a loose ball rolled onto her court, she would simply bat it out of the way in any direction at all instead of politely sending it back to the player it belonged to, as is done in tennis. But Althea had played in the street all her life and she just didn't know any better."

One of the days I remember best at the Cosmopolitan Club was the day Alice Marble played an exhibition match there. I can still remember saying to myself, boy, would I like to be able to play tennis like that! She was the only woman tennis player I'd ever seen that I felt exactly that way about. Until I saw her, I'd always had eyes only for the good men players. But her effectiveness of strike, and the power that she had, impressed me terrifically. Basically, of course, it was the aggressiveness behind her game that I liked. Watching her smack that effortless serve, and then follow it into the net and put the ball away with an overhead as good as any man's, I saw possibilities in the game of tennis that I had never seen before.

It's a funny thing. I had no way of knowing then that when the time came for me to be up for an invitation to play at Forest Hills, my biggest support aside from a handful of my own people would be this same Alice Marble.

I began taking lessons from Fred Johnson in the summer of 1941, but it wasn't until a year later that he entered me in my first tournament. The American Tennis Association, which is almost all Negro, was putting on a New York State Open Championship at the Cosmopolitan Club, and Fred put me in the girls' singles. It was the first tournament I had ever played in, and I won it. I was a little surprised about winning, but not much. By this time I was accustomed to winning games. I think what mostly made me feel good was that the girl I beat in the finals, Nina Irwin, was a white girl. I can't deny that that made the victory all the sweeter to me. It proved to my own satisfaction that I was not only as good as she was, I was better.

Nina, incidentally, also took lessons from Fred Johnson, but I think he was pleased when I won. The other members had no choice; they had to like it. I won, didn't I? Actually, even though almost all the club members were Negro, a lot of them probably were rooting for Nina because they thought I was too cocky and they figured it would do me good to get beat. It's always been a fault of mine that I don't let many people get close to me, and not many of those people had any way of knowing what I was really like or what made me that way. I guess they do now. But in those days part of my defense was in being assertive and a show-off. Just the same, winning softened a lot of opinions about me. After I showed them the championship material that was in me, things changed noticeably around the club. I found that I was accepted solely on my merits, and my attitude toward people didn't seem to matter so much any more. Not many people, I've found out, find fault with a winner.

Later in the same year-the summer of 1942-the club took up a collection to send me to the A.T.A. national girls' championship at Lincoln University in Pennsylvania. That was my first national tournament, and I lost in the finals. The girl who beat me was Nana Davis, whose name is now Nana Davis Vaughan, and I think it's interesting to read what Nana said about that match to a reporter who talked to her after I won at Wimbledon:

"Althea was a very crude creature. She had the idea she was better than anybody. I can remember her saying, 'Who's this Nana Davis? Let me at her.' And after I beat I her, she headed straight for the grandstand without bothering to shake hands. Some kid had been laughing at her and she was going to throw him out."

There wasn't any A.T.A. national championship tournament in 1943 because of the war and the restrictions on travel, but I won the girls' singles in both 1944 and 1945, and then, when I turned eighteen, my life began to change. For one thing, the social workers I had been reporting to no longer had charge of me. I wasn't a minor any more. Of course, I no longer was in line for the allowance I had been getting, either, but that didn't seem so important stacked up against the fact that I was able to run my own life at last. I had made friends with a girl named Gloria Nightingale, and I went to live with her in her family's apartment. I got a job as a waitress and I paid rent to Gloria's grandmother.

Gloria and I had a lot of fun together. During the winter of 1945-46, we played on the same basketball team--it was called The Mysterious Five-and we used to play as many as four or five games a week against different industrial teams. Whenever we weren't playing basketball we went bowling. Sometimes, even though it meant that we wouldn't get home until three or four in the morning, we would go bowling after we had finished a basketball game. Gloria was like me; all she cared about was playing games and having a good time. I still consider those years the liveliest of my whole life. We were really living. No responsibilities, no worries, just balling all the time.

It was through Gloria that I met Edna Mae and Sugar Ray Robinson. Gloria had known Edna Mae for a long time, and one night when we were out bowling, we saw Ray in the place and she introduced me to him. To show you how cocky I was, I got on him right away. "So you're Sugar Ray Robinson?" I said. "Well, I can beat you bowling right now!" I think he took a liking to me right away. Anyway, from that night on, I used to go up to his place every chance I got. Whenever I could I would sleep there. Ray and Edna were real good friends; I felt that they liked me, and I was crazy about them. When Ray went into the army, I stayed with Edna a lot. I was what you might call her Girl Friday. I did everything I could to make our relationship a lasting one. When Ray was in training, I used to go and live with Edna in a place on the other side of the mountain from his camp at Greenwood Lake, New York. We used to take a long hike from our cottage to Ray's cabin-it must have been about three miles every morning, and that wonderful mountain air seemed great to a kid from 143rd Street. Not that there was anything the matter with the air in Harlem; it was just that there were an awful lot of people using it.

Both Edna and Ray were kind to me in lots of ways. They seemed to understand that I needed a whole lot of help. I used to love to be with them. They had such nice things. Sometimes they would even let me practice driving one of their fancy cars, even though I didn't have a license. I think it gave Ray a kick to see how much fun I got out of it.

Ray had a set of drums that he liked to play and I always had an inkling for music myself. My favorite instrument was the saxophone. I just loved the sound of it. One day I asked Edna if she thought Ray would buy me one, and she said the only way to find out was to ask him. So I did, and he told me that as long as I was really serious about it and not just fooling around, if I went to a music store or a hockshop and found one, he would pay for it. I asked a few people where I ought to go look and they said I should try down around Eighth and Ninth Streets and Third Avenue. I went down there and saw a beautiful sax in a pawnshop window, just exactly what I wanted. The man in the store said I could have it for hundred seventy-five, and I rushed back and told Ray. He seemed pretty skeptical. "A hundred and seventy-five dollars?" he said. "That sounds like a lot of money for a second-hand saxophone. I'll tell you what you do. You go find Buddy Walker and ask him to go down there with you. He knows the score. He can tell whether it's worth it or not." So I hurried out to find Buddy and got him to go with me to look at it. Buddy gave the pawnshop man a hard time. "What's the matter with you, trying to cheat a young girl like this?" he said. "You can see she doesn't know anything about it. I'm a musician myself. I'm tellin' you this thing isn't worth any more than a hundred dollars." The pawnbroker wouldn't go quite that far, but when Buddy showed him bis union card he did knock fifty dollars off the price, so I got it for one hundred twenty-five dollars, and Ray gave me the money right away, like he'd promised he would. I've never forgotten it, and, for that matter, I still have the sax, although I haven't tried to play it in a long time-which is a break for the neighbors. They're better off when I sing. I hope.

Being eighteen, I was able to play in the A.T.A. national women's singles in 1946; I was out of the girls' class. They played it at Wilberforce College in Ohio, and the A.T.A. paid my expenses out there and saw to it that I was put up in the college dormitory. I got to the finals and lost to Roumania Peters, a Tuskegee Institute teacher who was an experienced player; she had won the title in 1944. It was my inexperience that lost the match for me. Roumania was an old hand at tournament play and she pulled all the tricks in the trade on me. I wasn't ready for it. But I didn't feel too bad. There was no disgrace connected with losing in the finals.

I probably wouldn't have minded much at all if I hadn't felt so strongly that I had let Roumania "psych" me out of the match. I was overconfident, there's no doubt about it, and she really worked on me. She won the first set, 6-4, and after I pulled out the second, 9-7, she began drooping around the court as though she was half dead. She looked for all the world as though she was so exhausted, she couldn't stand up. Naturally, I thought I had it made. It was quite a shock to me when Roumania managed to keep running long enough to win the third set, 6-3. It was also a good lesson for me. Unhappily, some of the A.T.A. people who had come out from New York were pretty disappointed in me. Maybe they thought they hadn't got their money's worth out of me because I had lost. I remember one of them saying something to the effect that they were through with me, that they didn't think much of my attitude, and I know I was a pretty dejected kid for a while. But I had played well enough, anyway, to attract the attention of two tennis playing doctors, Dr. Hubert A. Eaton of Wilmington, North Carolina, and Dr. Robert W. Johnson of Lynchburg, Virginia, who were getting ready to change my whole life.

They thought I was a good enough prospect to warrant special handling. I've often wondered if, even then, at that early stage of the game, they were thinking in terms of me someday playing at Forest Hills or Wimbledon. Whether they were or weren't, they certainly were looking to the future. It was their idea that what I ought to do first was go to college, where I could get an education and improve my tennis at the same time. "There are plenty of scholarships available for young people like you," Dr. Eaton told me. "It wouldn't be hard at all to get you fixed up at some place like Tuskegee."

"That would be great," I told him, "except I never even been to high school."

That stopped them for a while, but the two doctors talked it over with some of the other A.T.A. people and decided that I was too good a tennis prospect to let go to waste. I suppose, now that I think hard on it, they already were hoping that I might just possibly turn out to be the Negro player they had been looking for to break into the major league of tennis and play in the white tournaments. Although they never said so to me-not for a long time, the plan they finally came up with was for me to leave New York City and go to Wilmington to live with Dr. Eaton during the school year, go to high school there, and practice with him on his private backyard tennis court. In the summer I would live with Dr. Johnson in Lynchburg and I would travel with him in his car to play the tournament circuit. Each doctor would take me into his family as his own child and take care of whatever expenses came up during the part of the year I was with him. It was an amazingly generous thing for them to want to do, and I know I can never repay them for what they did for me.

Not that it was an easy decision for me to make. I was a city kid and I liked city ways. How did I know what it would be like for me in a small town, especially in the South? I'd heard enough stories-to worry me. Up north, the law may not exactly be on your side, but at least it isn't always against you just because of the color of your skin. I would have to go into this strange country, where, according to what I'd heard, terrible things were done to Negroes just because they were Negroes, and nobody was ever punished for them. I wasn't at all sure going into something like that was a good idea. Harlem wasn't heaven but at least I knew I could take care of myself there. I might have turned down the whole thing if Edna and Sugar Ray hadn't insisted that I should go. "You'll never amount to anything just bangin' around from one job to another like you been doin'," Ray told me. "No matter what you want to do, tennis or music or what, you'll be better at it if you get some education." In the end I decided he was right, and I wrote Dr. Eaton and told him I was coming. That was in August, 1946. He wrote me back and said I should get there by the first week in September. It didn't even leave me time to change my mind.

3

LOOK AWAY, DIXIE LAND

I went back to my mother and father's apartment to pack for the trip south. I used two suitcases; all my tennis clothes went into one and all the rest of my things into the other. Both of them were made of cardboard and they surely would have fallen apart if I hadn't tightened a spare belt around each one of them. I splurged on a taxicab to carry me down to Pennsylvania Station, and I must have been a sight to behold when I walked into the waiting room with a suitcase in each hand and Sugar Ray's saxophone hanging from a strap around my neck. I was so nervous about the whole thing, it was a miracle I didn't just check the bags and the sax, turn in the ticket Dr. Eaton had sent me, and go back to Harlem to see the matinee show at the Apollo.

The ticket Dr. Eaton had bought for me was a coach fare, so I sat up all night on the trip from New York to Wilmington. For food, I bought peanut butter crackers, sandwiches and milk from the candy butcher who walked back and forth through the train. Every time I needed a dollar I reached for the little bankroll I had secured to the inside of my blouse with a great big safety pin. Fortunately, nobody sat next to me, so I was able to stretch out on the seat during the night and get a little sleep. Mostly, though, instead of sleeping, I just thought about what I was getting into. I thought about how lucky I was to be asked to live in a good home with people like the Eatons. I knew enough about the doctor to know that he was pretty well off financially and didn't lack for anything he wanted. I hoped I would do everything right, so they wouldn't be sorry they had started the whole thing. I made up my mind that I would adjust myself to whatever came along. But that didn't stop me from worrying about how it would be, about whether I would like it living in with the family, whether they would give me any money to spend on myself, would the movie houses refuse to let me in because I was colored, would I have to get off the sidewalk if a white person came along, and all kinds of things like that. By the time the conductor came through the car and called out, "The next station stop is Wilmington," I was as nervous as a cat. But when I got off and saw this neatly dressed chauffeur coming up to me, and heard him ask if I was Althea Gibson, I began to feel better. Then, when I leaned back against the cushions in the back seat of Dr. Eaton's big car, and thought, ain't this a blip, he sure has nice things, this shouldn't be too hard to take, I felt pretty good.

I must have given Mrs. Eaton a turn when I got out of the car and walked through the kitchen door.

I was wearing a tired old skirt that I had picked out because I figured it wouldn't matter if it got beat up on the train ride. I hated to wear anything except slacks, anyway, so I probably looked every bit as uncomfortable as I felt. I'd never owned a real dress since I'd been a little girl; a sweater and skirt combination was as far as I was willing to go in the direction of looking feminine. But Mrs. Eaton didn't bat an eye. I'd never met her before but she hugged me and kissed me as though I were her favorite niece. She was busy getting lunch ready, but she took time out to introduce me to the Eaton children and the maid and to show me to my room. Then she asked me if I was hungry, and when I said yes, I hadn't eaten my breakfast, she invited me to help myself to whatever I saw in the icebox that looked good to me. I fixed a couple of eggs and some bacon, cleaned up after, then looked all around the house and admired how nice it was. It was a far cry from what I'd been used to. Everything was as clean and as fresh as it could be. I can still remember running my fingers across the clean, starched white sheets on my bed and thinking how nice it would be to get right into it.

I was still in my room, putting away my things, when Dr. Eaton came home from his office a little after three o'clock. He stood at the foot of the stairs and called up to me, "Althea! Althea!" I hurried out into the hall and said hello to him and said how beautiful my room was and how glad I was to be there, and he said, "You feel like hitting any, or are you too tired?" I said, "Oh, no, I feel fine. I'll be ready in a minute." And in just a few minutes I was out with the doctor on his handsome *en tout cas* court, trying to get a service ace past him, and my home life with the Eatons had officially begun.

The first big problem that had to be solved was where I would fit into the school. I didn't really have enough legitimate credits to get into the seventh grade, much less the second year of high school, which was what I hoped to talk my way into. But they gave me an aptitude test, and when they finished grading it they said they would assign me to the sophomore class and give me a chance to stick there if I could. That meant I would be able to earn my diploma in three years, and I was determined to do it. I buckled down to my schoolwork like nobody's business. I don't mean I was an angel. I still ducked off to the poolroom every chance I got, to relax a little, but I really hit those books.

Gradually, living in Dr. Eaton's house as one of the family, I learned how to obey rules and get along with people. It was the first real family life I had ever known. Nobody stayed out all night in that house or decided to eat lunch in a dog wagon downtown instead of coming home for lunch with the family. And the rules that applied to the Eatons' own children applied to me, too. I even got an allowance every week, the same as they did, so I could see that the good came with the bad. Not that there was anything bad about it, it was just that I wasn't used to living according to somebody else's plan. I'd been on my own for so long that I chafed under the discipline. Sometimes, naturally, I felt like rebelling, like doing what I wanted to do for a change. It just wasn't in me to be that good all the time. But, thank God, I never did anything really bad. I guess the worst thing I ever did was the night I borrowed Dr. Eaton's mother's car.

I'd joined the Williston Industrial High School band, and, through that, I'd got in with a group of fellows who had a little jazz combo that played gigs here and there around town for pocket money. The trumpet player had a big eye for me, and I liked him, too. Well, this night, Dr. and Mrs. Eaton went out with the doctor's mother, who left her car in the driveway. I was doing some homework up in my room and I kept looking out the window at that car, thinking how easy it would be to take off for a little joyride and come back before the doctor came home. Nobody, I figured, would ever be the wiser. I should have known better but I finally yielded to temptation. I'd seen where Mrs. Eaton had left her keys, so I ran downstairs and grabbed them and took off. I headed right across town to this trumpet player's house and tooted the horn until he came out. We went for a quick ride, parked a few times and did a little necking, and then I dropped him off and shot back to the Eatons' as fast as I could. I was relieved to see that the doctor hadn't come back yet, and I parked the car exactly where Mrs. Eaton had left it. But I might have known I wouldn't get away with it. Somebody saw me and told the doctor. The next morning he called me, and I could tell right away he was angry. "Althea," he said, "did you take my mother's car out last night?" I didn't see any point in lying to him. "Yes, sir," I said, pretty sheepishly. "You're aware that you don't have a license, aren't you?" he said, real mad. I just stood there and looked at my feet. 'Tm sorry, Doctor," I said. "I just thought I'd take a little spin and come right back." He was so angry he just walked away from me, and I guess I came pretty close to being sent away from there that very day. Dr. Eaton had no intention of letting me mess up things for his family. But he must have made up his mind that I'd had a good scare and wouldn't be likely to do anything else like that again, because he never said anything more about it.

I tried to make sure he would never be sorry he had given me another chance. I worked hard on both my schoolwork and my tennis. I think the doctor was proud of what I did with both. I'm sure he was pleased with my tennis. He loved to see me beat the men he matched me against. His court was a gathering place for all the Negro tennis players of the district, as it had to be, because there wasn't any place else for them to play. There were a number of public courts in Wilmington, but no Negro could play on them. I'm glad to say there were quite a few fine white players who came to Dr. Eaton's to play with the good Negro players, and I often heard some of them criticize the stupidity of the segregation laws that kept them from playing together on the public courts. "There's no sense in it," I remember one white man grumbling, "no sense in it at all." I agreed with him but I kept my mouth shut about it because I knew it would only embarrass Dr. Eaton if I started popping off in his home town. I'm sure things are no different there now than they were then.

The local segregation setup wasn't quite as bad as I had feared it might be, but it was plenty bad enough. I'll never forget my first bus ride into the downtown shopping area. The first thing I saw when I got on the bus and paid my fare was the sign, "White in front, Colored in rear." I was burned up that I had to conform to such an ignorant law, and I picked out a seat as near to the front as I thought I could possibly get away with. It disgusted me, and it made me feel ashamed in a way I'd never been ashamed back in New York.

It was even worse when I went to the movies. The ushers practically knocked us colored down making sure we got up to the back balcony, which was the only place in the whole theater we were allowed to sit. Actually, I've never liked to sit in the orchestra; I'll sit in the balcony every time I get the chance. But I never really enjoyed a movie all the time I was in the South because I had to sit in the balcony. There's a big difference between what you do because you want to and what you do because you're made to do it.

Then there was the thing about not being able to eat a hot dog at the food counter in the five-and-ten. You could buy one-they didn't mind taking your dime, no matter how black you were-but you had to take it out onto the street. You couldn't eat it in the store.

Of course, it was nothing more than I'd expected and, like I said, it wasn't a Ku Klux Klan nightmare like I'd been afraid it might be. I managed to conform to whatever I the program was wherever I went. But I hated every minute of it. I made up my mind once and for all that I was never going to live any place in the South, at least not as long as those laws were in existence. My daddy thinks I'm wrong. He says he would like nothing better than to go back to Silver, South Carolina, and raise chickens on the old farm place. He says things are already a lot better down there and they're going to get better all the time. "Anyway," he's always arguing with me, "a man can breathe fresh air in South Carolina. You can make a little dam in the brook and go for a good cold swim when it gets hot in the summertime. And at night, when you got all the work done, you can walk down the road and look at the stars and smoke a pipe and feel like you got a piece of the world to live in." Maybe he's got something there. When I say something about the Jim Crow, he points to the slum tenements in Harlem with the plaster falling down and the plumbing stopped up and the kids getting killed in the streets, and he says, Is this better? It makes you wonder what's right. But I still say I'll take Harlem, or worse, before I'll live somewhere where all the talent or brains or success in the world won't get you treated like anything except an untouchable if your skin happens to be dark. You can have my share of the South-if you want it. The only reason I would ever go there would be to visit with the people I care about.

The other big problem I had in Wilmington was the girls in school. Most of them didn't like me at all. I'm not sure if maybe it wouldn't be more accurate to say they didn't understand me, but either way you put it, we didn't get along. I wasn't much for dressing up, even though Mrs. Eaton had bought me a few nice dresses and had had my hair curled and showed me how to put on lipstick. I still wore slacks and a T-shirt every chance I got, and because I loved to play basketball and baseball and football with the boys, all the girls thought I was the worst tomboy they'd ever seen. I was the star of the girls' basketball team, and later on they elected me the captain of it, but that wasn't enough athletic action to keep me happy, so I used to go out to the field during football and baseball practice and play with the varsity boys. It used to hurt me real bad to hear the girls talking about me when they saw me doing that. "Look at her throwin' that ball just like a man," they would say, and they looked at me like I was a freak. I hated them for it. I felt as though they ought to see that I didn't do the things they did because I didn't know how to, and that I showed off on the football field because throwing passes better than the varsity quarterback was a way for me to express myself, to show that there was something I was good at.

It seemed sometimes as though nobody could understand me. I've always liked to sing, and I went out for the school choir, figuring that that was one place where I ought to be able to fit in easily. But the instructor couldn't make up his mind what to do with me. First he put me in the alto section, but when he struck a chord and we began to sing in chorus, my voice sounded like a boy's in the middle of all the girls, and it ruined the whole thing. So the instructor said, "Well, let's try you in with the tenor boys. Maybe that'll work better." It did, as far as my singing was concerned, but the girls giggled so much about it that I got tired of it and quit.

At least I had my saxophone. I stayed in the marching band, and in the small jazz combo, as long as I was in school. There was no school tennis team, so I had to be satisfied with the tennis I played at Dr. Eaton's. Then, during the vacation months, I went to Lynchburg and spent the summer playing with Dr. Johnson. I really worked there. I practiced with a Tom Stowe Stroke Developer, a robot machine that fired tennis balls across the net at me in a steady stream, and with every player who was willing to get out on the court and take me on. I played in nine tournaments that first summer, 1947, and won the singles championship in every one. Dr. Johnson and I won eight mixed doubles tournaments. One of the singles titles I won was the biggest that was open to me, the A.T.A. national women's singles, which I took by beating Nana Davis, 6-3, 6-0. It was the first of ten straight years that I won it. For whatever it was worth, I was the best woman player in Negro tennis. Winning the championship got me three or four lines of type at the bottom of the page in the *New York Times*. *The New York Daily News*, which has less space, didn't mention it at all.

We had some good times making those summer tours of the A.T.A. circuit, although our traveling arrangements were far from luxurious. We would spend the early part of the summer practicing on Dr. Johnson's court, which, like Dr. Eaton's, was right back of his house. Then, along about the first of July, we would start to travel. It was a revelation to me the first year we did it. Dr. Johnson had a big

Buick and he packed six or seven of us in it, with our bags stuffed in the trunk and in a big luggage rack bolted on the roof. We played in Washington, Philadelphia, New York and New Jersey, and then we all jammed into the car and headed for Kentucky. Dr. Johnson wanted us to play in a little tournament down there; I think a friend of his was the manager. But the doctor had the good sense to fly ahead and let the rest of us come on in the Buick. There was Babe Jones, Bobbie Johnson, the doctor's son, Biddie Woods, Carl Williams, and, last but not least when it came to squeezing into the car, long-legged Althea. We went by way of Missouri, and stopped off to play a tournament in Kansas City. Hot? It was broiling. I remember it was 105 in Kansas City, and Babe Jones fainted on the court during one of his matches. We stayed in a Negro hotel there, and at night it was unbearable. We kept the fans going all night but it didn't help. We were glad to leave the state of Missouri and start out for Kentucky. It was a long ride, and we must have been about thirty minutes outside Louisville when we got a flat tire. Just then it began raining cats and dogs. The rain was nice because it cooled the air, but the boys couldn't get the tire changed and we had to spend the whole night trying to sleep in the car. "You slept right on top of me," Biddie Woods always tells me whenever he sees me. And maybe I did. We were pretty well entangled in a bunch.

"Did you have a nice trip?" Dr. Johnson wanted to know when we called for him at the home of the man who was in charge of the tournament. He was always a card with the jokes.

We met Dr. Eaton at the A.T.A. nationals, which climaxed the season, and both the doctors were mighty pleased when I beat Nana to win it. I don't guess any of us had any idea I would win the thing ten years in a row. I finally stopped playing in it in 1957, partly because I was busy and partly because I wanted to give somebody else a chance. The A.T.A. people don't ask me to play in it any more. They would rather see their tournament develop some new champions and they would rather see me play in as many U.S.L.T.A. tournaments as I can, on the ground that that's more important to Negro tennis.

They didn't always feel that way, though. I remember one year there was a big fuss about it. I had won the A.T.A. six or seven times, and Dr. Eaton wanted me to play in the national women's doubles instead. The dates conflicted head on, so it had to be one or the other. "There's nobody here who can give her any competition anyway," Dr. Eaton said. "Let her go play in the doubles. Every U.S.L.T.A. tournament she plays in is a step forward." But some of the A.T.A. officials didn't see it that way at all. One of them said, "If she doesn't play in the A.T.A., we'll fix it so she doesn't play at Forest Hills any more, either." I doubt if he meant it, I think he was just working his points, but he did say it, and it just goes to show you that there can be prejudice and jealousy on both sides of the fence. I was lucky to have men like my two doctors looking out for me. Not only because they were doing so much for me in a material way, but because they were such high-type men. They're quite different, the two doctors, and yet they're very much alike. Dr.

Eaton is tall, about six feet, and slim; Dr. Johnson is short and husky. Dr. Eaton, who is a graduate of the University of Michigan, is a quiet kind of man who likes tennis, golf and photography; Dr. Johnson, whose nickname is Whirlwind, is an active sportsman who was a famous football player at Lincoln University when he was younger and who likes to fish and hunt and thinks nothing of driving a couple of hundred miles to see a good football game. Both of them are physician-surgeons with private clinics of their own, which is a common thing in Southern towns where Negro patients have to have a little clinic or hospital of their own because most of the time they aren't allowed in the white hospitals. And last but not least, both of the doctors are ardent poker players.

As far as I'm concerned, one of the best hands of poker they ever played was dealing me into the big leagues of tennis. Even today I'm hazy on all the details of the arrangements, but I guess what happened was that the top officials of the A.T.A., men like Bertram Baker and Arthur Francis, had made up their minds that the time had come to press as hard as they could for the acceptance of a qualified Negro player into the U.S.L.T.A. setup. They felt that the time was right, historically, and they felt that in me they had the key they had been looking for to open the door. They hadn't wanted to kick up a fuss until they knew they had a player good enough to back up their argument. For a long time, they had been hoping that I would be the one. Now they were sure I could do it, and they were ready to move.

The first I heard about it was when Dr. Eaton sat down next to me at the A.T.A. championships in the summer of 1949 and said, very casually, "Althea, how would you like to play at Forest Hills?"

All I said was, "Huh! Who you kidding?" He knew I would give my right arm to play against the white girls and knew that I knew he knew it. I had talked about it often enough, although never as a genuine possibility, just as something that rankled me and ate at me.

"Well," he said, grinning a little like a cat who knows where the bottle of cream is, "I'm not saying for sure you're going to, but I'll say this much. It could happen. People are working on it."

"I'm ready," I told him. "I'm ready any time they are." One thing that was working for us was the simple fact that tennis is a gentleman's game, and a lady's game. Tennis people, by and large, are decent people, mannerly people. They knew that Jackie Robinson had been playing baseball for the Brooklyn Dodgers for two seasons, that other Negro players were coming into the game in a steady stream, and that it was obvious that a great social change was in the making in this country. They listened politely while Mr. Baker and his associates talked about what they wanted to do. Maybe some of them were reluctant to see it happen, but most of them were men and women of good will. They said it sounded reasonable and they would see what could be worked out. My first break came when the A.T.A. was notified that if I sent in an entry form for the Eastern Indoor Championships, to be played right in my old backyard in the armory at 143rd

Street and Fifth Avenue, I would be accepted. It was an especially good break for me because I was familiar with the surroundings and not likely to feel particularly strange. I'd played at the armory lots of times in the last three or four years, whenever I had been around New York in the wintertime and happened to have enough money to pay the fee. The A.T.A., of course, was tremendously excited about the opportunity, and so was I. I did all right in the tournament. I played pretty well before Betty Rosenquest put me out in the quarter-finals 8-6, 6-0 and I was reasonably satisfied. At least I hadn't been disgraced.

I felt even better when I was asked, right after my last match, if I would like to stay over in New York for another week and play in the National Indoor Championships. Naturally, I wanted to very much, and all the A.T.A. people wanted me to; it was exactly the kind of progress they had been hoping for. So, they fixed it with the principal of Williston High, and I put in my entry blank. I wasn't, incidentally, the first Negro ever to play in the National Indoors. Dr. Reginald Weir of New York had beaten me to that distinction by a couple of years. But I felt that I was on my way, that I was getting my fair chance, and I couldn't ask for anything more than that.

Once again, I lasted until the quarter-finals. I beat Ann Drye 6-0, 6-1 in the first round, and Sylvia Knowles 6-4, 3-6, 6-1 in the second. Then Nancy Chaffee, the pretty California girl who later married Ralph Kiner, the ballplayer, got hold of me and put me out of the tournament. But I was glad I had lasted until the round of eight. I had been there, I had been invited to play with the white girls in one of the important tournaments, and I felt good about it. The world didn't have to reform overnight; I was willing to give it a few days.

In both the U.S.L.T.A. tournaments I played in that winter-my first experiences as the only Negro in an otherwise all-white draw-I was made to feel right at home by the other girls. It wasn't just that they were polite; they were genuinely friendly, and believe me, like any Negro, I'm an expert at telling the difference. It was as though they realized how much of a strain I was under, and they wanted to do whatever they could to help. Gussie Moran won the Indoors that year, and she couldn't have been nicer to me. I've come to know Gussie better since then, and I know she wasn't going through any diplomatic motions that first time; she's just that kind of girl. She was simply being natural. The whole experience gave me a lot of hope for the future, and a lot of confidence. Somewhat to my own surprise, because I'd had so little to do with books before I went to Wilmington, I finished up my high school course in three years, just as I had hoped I might be able to, and was graduated, in June, 1949, tenth in my class if you please. I was happy about it. I was twenty-one years old and I felt it was time I set out on my own. Partly I was ready to break loose and have a little fun, but partly I was dead serious about making something out of my life.

I remember a thing that happened around graduation time. All the girls in the senior class were ordering their class rings, and I wanted one badly. But I hated to ask Dr. Eaton for the money; they cost fifteen dollars, and it didn't seem fair to ask a man who had put out so much money for me already to buy something I didn't really need. So I sat down and wrote a few letters to people back in New York who I thought might be willing to help me, and I asked them if they could send me something toward the cost of the ring. The only one I ever heard from was Sugar Ray Robinson, and he sent me the whole fifteen dollars.

My last month in Wilmington I wrote letters to a number of Negro colleges, asking what chance I might have of getting a scholarship. As the two-time winner of the national Negro women's tennis championship, I had a pretty good claim. One of the schools that encouraged me was Florida A&M at Tallahassee. In fact, they did more than encourage me. Even before I got my high school diploma they wrote and said I was welcome to a scholarship at A&M, and that I should come down as soon as I got out of high school and spend the summer playing tennis down there. I had my bags packed two days after graduation, and I was gone. I'm afraid the Eatons were a little bit hurt about the speed with which I left, but I couldn't help being eager to get started on my own. Nobody could have been more grateful than I was to both the doctors for everything they had done for me in those three years, but it was good to feel a little bit independent again. It's a feeling I've always been partial to.

4

COLLEGIATE!

Life at Florida A&M wasn't exactly like the campus life I had always seen portrayed in the movies, but it wasn't bad, either. I had been awarded a scholarship by Dr. William Gray, the president, after the tennis coach, Walter Austin, had recommended me for it. The scholarship paid for my room in the girls' dormitory, my books and my tuition. Jake Gaither, the athletic director, fixed me up with a job as assistant to the head of the women's physical education department, and the forty dollars a month I earned was enough to keep me in spending money. Not that there was much I could do with the money. There weren't many places in Tallahassee where the students were allowed to go, and mostly we got along with a radio in our room, dances every now and then in the college gym, and movies in the auditorium. We were better off going to our own movies because there was only one theater in town that would let Negroes in and that was the one that had nothing but second-run features. There was also a canteen on the campus where we could go to play pinochle, shoot a little pool, eat hamburgers and drink Cokes, and there was one off-campus eating place we were allowed to go to at specified hours. You could get a bottle of beer there, or a drink, and there was a jukebox, although you couldn't dance. If you were a senior, you could stay out as late as eleven o'clock; freshmen had to be in by nine.

Of course, there were plenty of opportunities for girls and their boy friends to sneak off by themselves. But if you were caught anywhere except where you had said you were going when you wrote your name in the sign-out book, you were a cinch to be hauled before the judiciary committee. One year, believe it or not, I was the chairman of the committee. And actually we were probably tougher on the kids than the teachers would have been. We thought nothing of restricting an offender to the campus for a couple of weeks.

I suppose one reason why I took a more serious view of college life than some of the other students did was the small matter of four or five years that I had on them. I was twenty-two years old when I first stuck my head in a classroom at A&M, in September 1949, and I was twenty-five when I graduated. I always thought of myself as a sort of aunt to the other kids. I became a member of Alpha Kappa Alpha sorority, but I didn't go much for the kid stuff about pledges being "slaves" to the members. It's a wonder, now that I look back on it, that I survived the pledge days at all.

It's funny, the things you remember. One of my principal memories of college is the way we had to dress up in black or navy-blue suits, with white blouses, three times a week for chapel services- and sometimes twice on Sundays. We thought it was ridiculous, and we used to gripe about it like a bunch of soldiers put on KP.

I got kind of a head start at A&M by taking some summer courses during the summer of 1949, before my freshman year officially began. The extra credits were helpful, and, as I said before, I enjoyed the feeling of being off by myself, on my own. Naturally, I took time out to travel to a few A.T.A. tournaments, including the national championships, where I won the women's singles for the third year in a row. But otherwise I stayed close to the campus until, early in 1950, I was invited to play again in the National Indoors. This time I went all the way to the finals before Nancy Chaffee, for the second straight year, knocked me out. She didn't fool around, either, this time; she really walloped me 6-2, 6-0. But, win, lose or draw, it was good experience for me, and even just getting to the finals was more than I had hoped for. When I got off the train at Tallahassee, going back to school, I got a welcome I'll never forget. You would have thought for sure I had won the tournament instead of losing it. The whole school marching band was out to play the alma mater when I stepped off the train, and even the acting president of the college was there to shake my hand. They had put up a big sign, 'Welcome Home, Althea!" on the campus, and altogether, for a freshman, it was a real big thing. I was overwhelmed, and very happy. Obviously, they all felt that what I had done was important not just to me but to all Negroes.

I have never regarded myself as a crusader. I try to do the best I can in every situation I find myself in, and naturally I'm always glad when something I do turns out to be helpful and important to all Negroes- or, for that matter, to all Americans, or maybe only to all tennis players. But I don't consciously beat the drums for any special cause, not even the cause of the Negro in the United States, because I feel that our best chance to advance is to prove ourselves as individuals. That way, when you are accepted, you are accepted voluntarily, because people appreciate you and respect you and want you, not because you have been shoved down their throats. This doesn't mean that I'm opposed to the fight for integration of the schools or other movements like that. It simply means that in my own career I try to steer clear of political involvements and make my way as Althea Gibson, private individual. I feel that if I am a worthy person, and if I have something worthwhile to contribute, I will be accepted on my own merits, and that is the way I want it.

Of course, acceptance doesn't always come easily, which is probably the understatement of the century. Back in 1950 I had the notion that, having done so well in the Indoors, I would almost as a matter of course be invited to play in the summer grass-court tournaments, the big ones. But nothing happened. The U.S.L.T.A. acted as though I wasn't there. It began to look, as spring rolled on into summer, as though I was going to be like the girl Pearl Bailey sings about, strictly an indoor girl. Outdoors I was a wallflower.

The newspapers began to pay a little attention to the situation because they sensed that if nobody allowed me to play on grass all summer, I almost certainly wouldn't be permitted to play at Forest Hills in September. If they didn't want me, if they were determined to keep me out, it would be easy enough for them to say that I hadn't proved myself on grass and that until I did I couldn't very well be invited to Forest Hills. But the newspapers began to ask, if I wasn't given a chance to play, how could I ever prove myself? The trouble was, nobody at Seabright, East Hampton, Newport, or in the offices of the U.S.L.T.A. seemed to be listening. Then, without any warning at all, a powerful champion struck a blow in my behalf. Alice Marble, still recognized as one of the greatest women tennis players the country ever produced, wrote an editorial in the July 1950, issue of *American Lawn Tennis* magazine. It kicked up a storm from one end of the tennis world to the other. This is what Miss Marble wrote:

"On my current lecture tours, the question I am most frequently expected to answer is no longer: 'What do you think of Gussie's panties?' For every individual who still cares whether Gussie Moran has lace on her drawers, there are three who want to know if Althea Gibson will be permitted to play in the Nationals this year. Not being privy to the sentiments of the U.S.L.T.A. committee, I couldn't answer their questions, but I came back to New York determined to find out. When I directed the question at a committee member of long standing, his answer, tacitly given, was in the negative. Unless something within the realm of the supernatural occurs, Miss Gibson will not be permitted to play in the Nationals.

"He said nothing of the sort, of course. The attitude of the committee will be that Miss Gibson has not sufficiently proven herself. True enough, she was a finalist in the National Indoors, the gentleman admitted-but didn't I think the field was awfully poor? I did not. It is my opinion that Miss Gibson performed beautifully under the circumstances. Considering how little play she has had in top competition, her win over a seasoned veteran like Midge Buck seems to me a real triumph.

"Nevertheless the committee, according to this member, insists that in order to qualify for the Nationals, Miss Gibson must also make a strong showing in the major Eastern tournaments to be played between now and the date set for the big do at Forest Hills. Most of these major tournaments -- Orange, East Hampton, Essex, etc. -- are invitational, of course. If she is not invited to participate in them, as my committee member freely predicted, then she obviously will be unable to prove anything at all, and it will be the reluctant duty of the committee to reject her entry at Forest Hills. Miss Gibson is over a very cunningly-wrought barrel, and I can only hope to loosen a few of its staves with one lone opinion.

"I think it's time we faced a few facts. If tennis is a game for ladies and gentlemen, it's also time we acted a little more like gentlepeople and less like sanctimonious hypocrites. If there is anything left in the name of sportsmanship, it's more than time to display what it means to us. If Althea Gibson represents a challenge to the present crop of women players, it's only fair that they should meet that challenge on the courts, where tennis is played. I know those girls, and I can't think of one who would refuse to meet Miss Gibson in competition. She might be soundly beaten for a while but she has a much better chance on the courts than in the inner sanctum of the committee, where a different kind of game is played.

"I can't honestly say that I believe Miss Gibson to be a potential champion; I don't know. In the Indoors she played under tremendous pressure, but there were moments when she exhibited a bold, exciting game that will doubtlessly improve against first-class competition. Whether she can achieve championship status here or abroad depends no more on her lovely strokes than on what Althea Gibson finds within herself when the chips are down. If she can do it, a proud new chapter will have been added to the history of tennis. If she cannot, we will have seen nothing more and nothing less than one more youngster who failed to live up to her initial promise. But if she is refused a chance to succeed or to fail, then there is an uneradicable mark against a game to which I have devoted most of my life, and I would be bitterly ashamed.

"We can accept the evasions, ignore the fact that no one will be honest enough to shoulder the responsibility for Althea Gibson's probable exclusion from the Nationals. We can just 'not think about it.' Or we can face the issue squarely and honestly. It so happens that I tan very heavily in the summer-but I doubt that anyone ever questioned my right to play in the Nationals because of it. Margaret

DuPont collects a few freckles-but who ever thought to omit her name for such a reason? The committee would have felt pretty foolish saying, 'Alice Marble can't play because of that tan,' or 'We can't accept Margaret DuPont; she gets freckles across her nose.' It's just as ridiculous to reject Althea Gibson on the same basis-and that's the truth of it. She is not being judged by the yardstick of ability but by the fact that her pigmentation is somewhat different.

"If the field of sports has got to pave the way for all of civilization, let's do it. At this moment tennis is privileged to take its place among the pioneers for a true democracy, if it will accept that privilege. If it declines to do so, the honor will fall to the next generation, perhaps but someone will break the ground. The entrance of Negroes into national tennis is as inevitable as it has proven to be in baseball, in football, or in boxing; there is no denying so much talent. The committee at Forest Hills has the power to stifle the efforts of one Althea Gibson, who may or may not be the stuff of which champions are made, but eventually she will be succeeded by others of her race who have equal or superior ability. They will knock at the door as she has done. Eventually the tennis world will rise up en masse to protest the injustices perpetrated by our policymakers. Eventually--why not now?

"I am beating no drums for Miss Gibson as a player of outstanding quality. As I said, I have seen her only in the National Indoors, where she obviously did not play her best and was still able to display some lovely shots. To me, she is a fellow tennis player and, as such, deserving of the same chance I had to prove myself. I've never met Miss Gibson but, to me, she is a fellow human being to whom equal privileges ought to be extended.

"Speaking for myself, I will be glad to help Althea Gibson in any way I can. If I can improve her game or merely give her the benefit of my own experiences, as I have many other young players, I'll do that. If I can give her an iota more of confidence by rooting my heart out from the gallery, she can take my word for it: I'll be there."

Right after Miss Marble's editorial appeared, I tried to enter the New Jersey State Championships at the Maplewood Country Club, but was refused. "Not enough information," was the reason they gave. In tennis parlance, that means the applicant hasn't played in enough recognized tournaments to qualify. There was no doubt about that, but the sixty-four dollar question was how was I going to be able to provide "enough information" if they didn't let me play in any of their tournaments? I have to admit I was beginning to get discouraged. Then, all of a sudden, the dam broke. The Orange Lawn Tennis Club in South Orange, New Jersey, one of the major clubs on the Eastern circuit, accepted my entry for the important Eastern Grass Court Championships. This was a major league tournament, second in importance on the Atlantic Seaboard only to the Nationals. It looked very much as though I had made it, as though the color line was broken. All I had to do was make a reasonably good showing and I would be sure to be accepted at Forest Hills. I was something less than a sensation, but I beat Virginia Rice Johnson in the first round before

Helen Pastall Perez put me out in the second. Next, I played in the National Clay Courts Championships at Chicago and got to the quarter-finals before Doris Hart put me out 6-2, 6-3. After that, Harold LeBair of the U.S.L.T.A. passed the word to Mr. Baker that if I applied for entrance into the Nationals, I would be accepted. I filled out the entry blank as fast as I could get hold of one.

Arthur Francis, a Brooklyn real estate man who was the assistant executive secretary of the A.T.A., and who was chiefly responsible for getting me into the Eastern Grass Courts, wrote a couple of interesting letters that summer. One of them went to James B. Dickey of the Eastern Lawn Tennis Association, thanking the E.L.T.A. for inviting me to play in its championship tournament. "Negroes will be everlastingly grateful to you and your colleagues who thought as you did and who by their actions have attested to the fact that tennis is a game for ladies and gentlemen, and of ladies and gentlemen," he said. In the other letter, written to the officials of the New Jersey association who had refused to let me play in the state tournament, he said, "You have exhibited the very thing that you apparently seemed to be afraid of in other people; snobbishness, prejudice and bad judgment--an un-American spirit that should not find its way in any respectable sport, particularly tennis, a game for ladies and gentlemen."

The big news came in the middle of August, and although the U.S.L.T.A. announced it in a very matter-of-fact fashion, there was nothing matter of fact about it to me. Lawrence A. Baker, who was the president of the association that year, said that I was one of the fifty-two women whose entries had been accepted for the national championship tournament, and he added meaningfully, "Miss Gibson has been accepted on her ability." That was all I had ever asked.

Once I knew that I was going to play at Forest Hills I began to worry about how I would react to playing in such an impressive place, a place I had never even seen. Somebody who knew Sarah Palfrey Cooke suggested that I call her and ask her if she would take me out there and practice with me, in order to give me a chance to get used to the place. Sarah was wonderful. She said she would be glad to, and she called Ralph Gatcomb, who was the president of the West Side Tennis. Club that year and asked him if it would be all right to bring me out for some practice. You have to remember that Sarah herself wasn't a member of the club, so it would have been easy for Mr. Gatcomb to say that he was sorry, but it wasn't allowed. But he didn't say anything of the kind. He said they would be happy to have me and he was glad Sarah had suggested it. So, I went out and practiced for a couple of hours with Sarah, and kind of got the feel of the place, and it was a big help. For that matter, just playing with Sarah was a big help. She's one of the finest tennis players I've ever had the pleasure of hitting against. She knows everything about tennis strokes and strategy that's worth knowing.

I stayed at Rhoda Smith's house on 154th Street in Harlem for the time at the Nationals, and I'll never forget the first day out there. Mrs. Smith and I got up early and ate a good breakfast, bacon and eggs and toast and milk, and then I got my things ready. I packed a small kit bag with a pair of tailored white flannel shorts, a flannel shirt, sweat socks, tennis shoes and a white knitted sweater that one of the A.T.A. ladies had made for me. I was ready. Rhoda and I walked to the Sixth Avenue Subway station, me carrying my bag in one hand and two tennis rackets in the other. We took a D train to 50th Street and Sixth Avenue, then changed to an F train, the express to Forest Hills, and got off at 71st Street and Continental Avenue. It was only a short walk, about three long blocks, to the entrance of the West Side Tennis Club. I couldn't help but think that it had taken me a long time to make the trip. A registration table had been set up on the front lawn, just inside the gate, and I stopped there to pick up my player's credentials. My fee for the singles had been paid in advance, but I also was going to play in the mixed doubles with Torsten Johansson of Sweden, and I had to pay the entry fee for that event. After the business was transacted, I walked into the clubhouse and downstairs to the ladies' dressing room. I was glad I'd already been there once with Sarah and knew my way around. I would have hated it if I'd had to ask directions.

Rhoda stayed with me while I changed into my tennis clothes, and it was a good thing she did. There were reporters and photographers all around, clamoring for interviews and pictures. I wouldn't have been able to cope with them all alone. The whole thing awed me. All this attention, all these people wanting to talk to me and get me to say things, patting me on the back and telling me that they knew I could do it-it was hard for a girl who had never been through the mill before. Being a close-mouthed person by nature, I couldn't help wishing they would all go away and leave me alone. But I did my best to go along with the program.

My first-round match was scheduled for one o'clock, so even though I got to the clubhouse a couple of hours early, I didn't eat anything before I played. The match, with Barbara Knapp of England, was an easy one, and after I'd won it 6-2, 6-2 I took a shower and got dressed and was escorted to one of the main clubhouse rooms for an interview with the press. I could have eaten lunch in the clubhouse then-in fact, a few of the U.S.L.T.A. officials, who probably wanted to be sure I understood that I was welcome, suggested it-but I was too excited to eat. I tried hard to be calm and poker-faced with the reporters, but I was pretty emotional deep down inside. I stayed around for a while, after the reporters had finished with me, and watched a few matches, then Rhoda and I walked back to the subway station and headed for home. We had an early dinner at Rhoda's that night, and I went to bed early. I would have liked to have gone to a movie, but I was afraid it might make my eyes tired, and I didn't want to take the chance.

There was quite a bit of comment in the newspapers that night to the effect that I had been discriminated against by the tournament committee when they assigned me to Court 14, which is the farthest removed from the clubhouse of all the courts on the club grounds and has the smallest capacity for accommodating spectators. It was pointed out in a lot of the stories that anybody could have foreseen that there would be a lot of spectator interest in my first match and that it was stupid to put me on a court where the scramble for a vantage point would be bound to cause unnecessary commotion. The writers also made a sarcastic point out of the fact that Ginger Rogers, the movie star, who could hardly have been considered a serious challenger, played her mixed doubles match on the court right in front of the clubhouse. But I didn't pay much attention to all that. I'd have been pretty backward if I didn't realize that Ginger Rogers was a far greater attraction for the people sitting on the clubhouse porch than Althea Gibson. I would have been far more interested in her myself, and I'm not joking. The only thing I did feel a little unhappy about, that first day, was the way the photographers kept exploding flash bulbs in my face while I was playing. I had understood that they weren't allowed to get so close to you during a match, and I wondered why the officials didn't give me a little more protection from them. But I didn't want to make any complaints, and anyway, I won the match.

The next day was the big one. My second-round opponent was Louise Brough, the Wimbledon champion and former champion of the United States. Louise was one of the big guns of women's tennis, and I could hardly ask for a better opportunity to show what I could do. I've always felt I did about as well as could be expected. Louise won the first set 6-1, and I suppose it's true, as almost all of the tennis writers reported, that I was very nervous. One of them said I looked "scared to death" out there. I think that was a slight exaggeration, but I'll cheerfully concede that I was tense. A heckler in the stands, who kept shouting "Knock her out of there! Knock her out of there!" didn't help me any. But in the second set I got hot. I took it 6-3 and I began to feel a lot more comfortable. I built up a 7-6 lead in the third set and was feeling real good about my chances when suddenly the courts were struck by a drenching thunderstorm, so violent that it knocked down one of the huge eagles that had stood at the comers of the stadium ever since it was built. They had to suspend play until the next day.

There is no doubt in my mind, or in anybody else's, that the delay was the worst thing that could have happened to me. It gave me a whole evening-and the next morning, too, for that matter-to think about the match.

By the time I got through reading the morning newspapers I was a nervous wreck. When I went out to the club that afternoon, I saw Sarah and asked her if she would practice with me for a while before the match was called, and she did. But I was still on edge when we began to play. I don't mean to overlook the fact that Louise was tense, too. After all, she was the champion of Wimbledon, and here she was in the position of losing one game and finding herself out of the tournament in the second round. But I think it's fair to say that the pressure on me was even worse.

We had a big gallery this time. Nobody wanted to miss it. In fact, it looked as though there were more newspapermen, photographers and newsreel cameramen around the court than spectators.

Actually, it lasted only eleven minutes. Louise served well, rushed to the net behind it, and got to 40-love in a hurry. I won the next two points on a clean return of service and a passing shot that caught Louise flatfooted at the net, but she caught my next service return for a beautiful half-volley and put it away for the game.

The next game was the best. I got into trouble right away. I gave Louise a setup off my forehand, double-faulted, won a point on an error, then hit a volley way out of the court. I was down 15-40. But I was determined not to give up without a fight. I picked up one point on a service ace and another on a kill shot at the net. Another volley gave me the advantage in the game. But then Louise passed me at the net with a hard crosscourt forehand, and we were all even again. We played exactly eighteen points before we settled the game, but in the end, it was Louise who won it. Now I was losing 8-7. Louise ran up a 40-15 lead in a hurry, on her own service, and it was match point. I saved it once with a lob that Louise hit out, but on her second try she hit. I hit a hard backhand that just went out, and Louise had won it 6-1, 3-6, 9-7.

Because I think it's important to have a completely objective report on something as meaningful as that match I played with Broughie, I would like to quote what David Eisenberg of the *New York Journal-American* said about it:

"I have sat in on many dramatic moments in sports, but few were more thrilling than Miss Gibson's performance against Miss Brough. Not because great tennis was played. It wasn't. But because of the great try by this lonely, and nervous, colored girl, and because of the manner in which the elements robbed her of her great triumph.

"Miss Gibson was terribly nervous when the match began, so that Miss Brough easily won the first set, 6-1. But Althea settled down in the second set. Rarely since Alice Marble's championship reign has a woman shown so much stroking power as she did, especially with her forehand. She won the second set, 6-3, and the match was squared.

"Miss Brough won the first three games of the final set. Again, Althea rallied, cracking Louise's service three times as she pulled ahead to a 7-6 lead while the skies became menacingly black, almost as dark as the night, with only lightning lighting up the clouds.

"The great Californian, the winner of the Wimbledon and National championships, was to serve next. But she was obviously very tired. The courage and the power of this unknown colored girl had robbed Louise of her poise. Everyone in the stands sensed that a fabulous upset was in the making. But it never came about. Ten minutes of thunder and lightning finally delivered the deluge. It poured, and the match ended as players, officials and spectators scurried to cover under the stands.

"The match was over until the next day, but not the tension for Althea Gibson. Now the press descended upon her in the marquee. It was a trying session for Miss Gibson, one made much more difficult by several members of her own race who decided to make themselves her personal protectors. One was a young man whom Althea later said she never had met before, another an unknown woman. Both tried to keep the press from talking with Althea, and bitter words were exchanged."

This much I can offer on my own. Believe me, it was a long ride back to Harlem on the subway that afternoon.

Before I went back to college I had lunch one day at the Crossroads Restaurant on 42nd Street and Broadway with Bertram Baker of the A.T.A. and Hollis Dann of the U.S.L.T.A. to talk about the possibilities of my playing at Wimbledon in the spring of 1951. The U.S.L.T.A. had no objections, but they weren't about to pay my way, either. However, they did suggest through Mr. Dann that, if I was serious about going, I ought to get a little more instruction, and they said they would arrange for me to go out to Hamtramck, Michigan, which is a suburb of Detroit, under their auspices, to work out with Jean Hoxie, one of the best-known tennis teachers in the country. I thought that was a fine idea, and in addition I was lucky enough to be invited to play in the Good Neighbor tournament at Miami, in March. I understand I was the first Negro player ever to compete in a mixed tournament anywhere in the Deep South. It was quite an experience. I felt as though I were on display, being studied through a microscope, every minute. When I first got to Miami, the tournament officials put me up at a very nice hotel on Miami Beach, the Admiral. I appreciated the gesture, and what it meant, but after I'd spent one night there I asked them to let me switch to the Mary Elizabeth, a hotel for Negroes in Miami proper. I was lonesome at the Admiral, all by myself. I'm an authority on what it feels like to be the only Negro in all-white surroundings, and I can assure you that it can be very lonely.

As soon as I finished my final exams at A&M that May, I flew out to Detroit. Bill Matney, a reporter for one of the Negro newspapers in Detroit, met me at the airport and took me to the Gotham Hotel, where the manager told me with a big smile that Joe Louis had left word with him that I was to use his personal suite while I was in town. So, I had nothing but the best, all for nothing, and I was glad I had a chance to tell Joe how much I appreciated it before I left for England. He bought me some breakfast one morning, talked to me about how I was doing, and told me he would have a round-trip airplane ticket to London left for me at Idlewild Airport in New York. What a guy.

I don't know how much I improved my tennis while I was in Detroit, but the Negro people there were wonderful to me. They even put on a benefit show at the Flame Show Bar and raised seven hundred and seventy dollars for me to use for hotels, meals and spending money on the trip to England. Before I left, Bill Matney took me into one of the downtown banks and drew out all the money that had been raised for me. Then he bought me a round-trip ticket to London and gave me the leftover cash. I didn't say anything about the ticket Joe had promised me because I was afraid maybe the champ would forget about it. But I should have known better. When I got to Idlewild, the ticket from Joe was there. So, I cashed in the one Bill Matney had bought for me, turned over the money to Bertram

Baker and asked him to keep it for me until I got back. I was flush.

Unfortunately, a pocketful of money wasn't enough to win for me at Wimbledon. All I got was more experience. Then it was back to another disappointing season in the United States, and a pattern had been set that was to last for a long time. I didn't advance in the game as fast as I had hoped I would, and certainly not as fast as a lot of people thought I should. Maybe I didn't get enough opportunities to play against topflight people. Whatever it was, the years 1951, '52 and '53 were mostly disappointing for me. Aside from the education I absorbed at Florida A&M, the only good things that happened to me were two wonderful friendships, one with a whole family and the other with a man who has been my coach and closest adviser ever since.

When the people who run the Eastern Grass Court Championships at East Orange invited me to play in their tournament for the second time in 1951, they unknowingly led me to a new home away from home. I needed a place to stay that would be reasonably close to the club. I was talking about it one day with some of the A.T.A. people and one man suggested that maybe Rosemary Darden, a good A.T.A. player I'd known for several years, who lived in Montclair, New Jersey, might be able to fix it for me to stay at her house. It sounded like a good idea, so the next time I saw Rosemary I asked her if she thought her mother would mind if I stayed with them for the week of the tournament. She said she would be glad to ask her, and she called home right then and there. At first Mrs. Darben, who wasn't feeling too well at the time, was afraid that she shouldn't do it because she didn't think she would be able to be a good hostess in her condition. But Rosemary said, "You don't have to worry about that with Althea, Mom. She's the down-to-earth type. You won't have to fuss over her." So that night I went over to the Darbens' and moved into Rosemary's room with her. I was the original man who came to dinner; they didn't get rid of me until seven years later.

I had, of course, intended to stay only for the week, but Rosemary and I got along wonderfully well together and she asked me to stay on for a while. It was all right with me. I was very happy there, not only because there really wasn't enough room for me in the apartment on 143rd Street, and not only because I liked it better out in the country where there was more air to breathe, but also because there were so many things Rosemary and I enjoyed doing together-tennis, golf, bowling, playing cards, listening to records. I just sort of grew into staying there permanently. Before I knew it I had moved in bag and baggage, and in fact, because my bags and baggage and trophies and scrapbooks and souvenirs and whatnot expanded so much over the years, in the end I almost succeeded in moving Rosemary out of her own room.

All the Darbens were like my own family to me, and I tried to be like family to them. For a while, as a matter of fact, it looked as though I might actually become a member of the family. One of the boys, William (there are three boys and three girls), started, after a few years, to take me out on dates. A lot of newspaper stories used to say we were engaged, but that isn't true. We went out together for several years, and William always used to meet me at the airport whenever I came home from a trip, which, I suppose, is why the reporters began to draw conclusions. But we never were engaged, and I never wore his ring. I thought seriously about him, but nothing ever came of it. I guess you could say there just wasn't any spark between us.

I still go to see the Darbens often, and I hope I will always be welcome there. Sometimes, when I'm telling them about some place I've just been, Mom Darben will interrupt and start teasing me. "Oh, my," she'll say, "when you first came in this house, you were just like a little mouse. We couldn't even get you to open your mouth. And look at you now." I always talk back and tell her, "I didn't say nothin' when I first came in here because I was scared. You looked so mean I was afraid to open my mouth." But she knows I don't mean what I say. She knows I love her and that I'm grateful to her for all the years she gave me a good home. I was happy there.

Getting together with Sydney Llewellyn, a Harlem tennis teacher who made ends meet by driving a taxicab, also has meant a lot to me. Not just because of what he did for me in a technical way, like changing my grip and instructing me in tactics, but in a mental way, too. He kept me interested in the game and kept urging me to make the most of the opportunity I had.

Aside from his wife, Leah, tennis is Sydney's whole life. I had known him since 1946 and had seen him around A.T.A. tournaments for years. Once, in 1950, we played mixed doubles together and were finalists in the New Jersey Open. Sydney came to me after he had read in *Jet* magazine an article labeling me "The Biggest Disappointment in Tennis." He urged me to let him coach me; he insisted that I could go all the way to the top. I liked his approach, he was so intense and so earnest, and I felt I could do well with him. He made me stop using the old-fashioned Continental grip, which allows you to hit both forehand and backhand with the same grip and which naturally enough was favored by Fred Johnson because he only had one arm. Syd also taught me a more limber stroke that enabled me to obtain a maximum use of my wrist in bringing the racket into contact with the ball. And he worked hard with me on court strategy, teaching me what he calls his "Theory of Correct Returns." I spent hours on the court with him, a bushel basket full of balls lying all around us, practicing my serve and my net game. Syd did a lot for me. The A.T.A. seemed to have lost interest in me, and I can't say I blamed them much. I kept on winning their tournament every year, but I was no bargain in U.S.L.T A. competition. I was ranked No. 9 nationally in 1952 and moved up to No. 7 in 1953, but I fell all the way down to No. 13 in 1954, and you can't call that progress.

That 1954 ranking was based, of course, on my play in the '53 tournaments, and that was the year I graduated from Florida A&M. and, through the good graces of our athletic director, Jake Gaither, got a job in the physical education department of Lincoln University at Jefferson City, Missouri. I taught there for two years, in '54 and '55, and it was quite an experience. For one thing, I had a wingding of a time with a wonderful man while I was there, and I wouldn't have missed that for the world. He was a captain in the army, and he was in charge of the ROTC unit on the campus. He was quite a few years older than I was, but I was such an innocent about everything that it was probably a good thing. On account of him, I almost gave up tennis for good.

I was discouraged, anyway, not doing any better than I was, still champion of nothing but the A.T.A., and I didn't see any way that things were likely to get better. I was tired of never having any money. My pay at Lincoln was only two thousand and eight hundred dollars my first year, and an even three thousand dollars the second year. I had a little apartment that cost me forty-eight dollars and fifty cents a month, and a secondhand Oldsmobile that I was paying for on time, and it didn't look like I'd ever be able to put anything by. When my captain friend began selling me on the idea of joining the Women's Army Corps, I listened mighty carefully. After all, a Wac could make enough money, if she had a college education and could become an officer, to live nicely, send something home to the family, and save something, too. The idea of being regimented and kept under discipline didn't worry me any; I'd been living like that for years. The more I thought about it the more I thought it was a good idea. Anyway, it might mean I could stay with the captain for a long time, and that interested me a lot.

Being in love, and being loved by somebody, was something brand new to me. Except for the kid stuff with the trumpet player in Wilmington, I'd had almost no experience with boys. And this would have been different, anyway, because my captain was no boy; he was forty-one years old, very much a grown man. I was twenty-six myself but, although I was mature and worldly-wise in most respects, I knew less about this subject than the average high school girl. That didn't stop me, though, from pretending to a knowledge and a sophistication I didn't possess.

It's funny, but the things that have seemed most important to you can suddenly become very unimportant compared with being with, and pleasing, somebody you love. Tennis no longer seemed like everything in the world to me; I was much more interested in going out on dates and having a good time. If the man in question had been closer to my own age, I probably would have become much more deeply involved, and maybe I really might have given up tournament tennis altogether. But two things worked against it. There was the captain's feeling that he was too old for me, and there was the nagging doubt in me about giving up on something I'd put so many years and so much sweat into. Not to mention what other people had put into it. In the end, we both decided we had to be satisfied with being friends. I won't go so far as to say I was satisfied, but I admit I went along with the decision. Tennis still had that big a hold on me.

The segregation in Missouri, coming on top of what I'd had to put up with all the years I was going to college in Tallahassee, had a lot to do with my considering the Wac seriously enough to actually send in an application. The people who lived in Jefferson City-the Negroes, I mean-didn't seem to mind it so much, but it bothered me all the time. I couldn't be complacent about it; I wasn't ready for that yet. I remember how aggravated I was one time when Donald McMoore, one of our Phys Ed teachers, and I decided to try to find a place near the college where we could go bowling, and where we could take some of our students to bowl. The first place we tried said no right away, nothing doing. But the man who owned the second place said it would be all right with him if we came only in the morning and left no later than half past one or two o'clock in the afternoon. That way, we would be out of the place before his regular customers showed up. We didn't particularly care for the rules, but we wanted to bowl, and he seemed like a decent sort of man, so we started going there. We had a lot of fun, too. We brought a few of the kids from the college with us, and we all enjoyed it. Then one day we walked into the place and a different man was behind the counter. He wanted to know what we were after, and when we told him we wanted to bowl, he got real nasty.

"Not in this place," he said. "No colored allowed to bowl here. This is for whites only." We tried to explain to him that we'd been bowling there for a long time, but he didn't care what we'd been doing. I finally went outside and called up the man we'd been dealing with, but he just said this fellow was his partner and he'd made up his mind to throw us out because some of the whites were complaining about us using the place in the morning. "I'm sorry," he said, and I think he meant it. "It's a matter of dollars and cents. If a couple of the leagues that use the place cancel out, we'll be in trouble. We can't afford to take the chance." And so ended our short experiment in sociological pioneering.

Finding enough to do in Lincoln was hard, no matter how you looked at it. It wasn't exactly New York, not by a long shot. Sports provided the best answer, and I played tennis and ping-pong and badminton, and I pitched and played the outfield for the faculty softball team. I was the only woman player on the team. I wanted to play on the faculty basketball team, too, but the men wouldn't let me; they said I might get hurt. The most they would let me do was work out with the varsity in practice. Dwight Reed, who is the head of the Phys Ed department out there, told a reporter last year: "You had to look two or three times at Althea to convince yourself that she was a girl. She played all the games so well. You couldn't tell she was a girl by the way she pitched or the way she shagged fly balls in the outfield."

Along with athletics, I spent a lot of my spare time playing bridge. I belonged to the Just-Us Bridge Club and the Playmore Duplicate Bridge Club, and I enjoyed that a lot. But it was much too quiet a life for me. They used to put out the lights and pull in the sidewalks at nine o'clock in Jefferson City, and if I wanted to go to the movies twice in the same week, I had to see the same picture over again. It was very unexciting.

When the 1955 school year ended, I packed my bags and went back to Harlem in the Oldsmobile and told Syd about the Wac application. He almost had a fit. He pleaded with me by the hour. He kept saying I was throwing away a chance at the best tennis career any woman had had since Helen Wills. (I thought he was giving me quite a bit the best of it there.) He did write a letter of character reference to support my application, but he made it plain that his heart wasn't in it. When I stopped by one day to tell him I had passed the physical and was just waiting for the call to go, he looked like I'd hit him over the head with a hammer. We weren't even playing much tennis anymore. There didn't seem to be I much point in it. But as the weeks went by and I still didn't hear from the army, I began to play a little bit I again, and I humored Syd by sending in my entry for the Nationals.

We were sitting in my car outside the courts at 150th Street and Seventh Avenue one afternoon when Syd said, "I can't get it through my head why you would do this. You got a great future in front of you."

"I don't see it," I said. "If I was any good I'd be the champ now. But I'm just not good enough. I'm probably never going to be. And I'm sick of having people support me, taking up collections for me, and buying me clothes and airplane tickets and every damn thing I eat or wear. I want to take care of myself for a change. In the army, I can do it."

"You can do it in tennis, too," Syd insisted. He was stubborn. But I argued him back. "Look," I said, "you think so, and maybe I think so, too. But we're the only ones who do, and we're only two people, and neither one of us has any money. We've had it." I meant it, too. Even when I got ready to play at Forest Hills again, my mind wasn't on the tennis. It had taken a long time, but I was sick of it. I think the only thing I really felt bad about was Syd. My making it meant a whole lot to him. There he was, pushing that taxicab through the New York traffic all day, trying to make a hard dollar so he could realize his dream of becoming a tennis pro. If I quit I wasn't just quitting on myself, I was quitting on him, too. Not that he wouldn't make it on his own anyway, because he would; he's that kind of man. But I could have been a good advertisement for him.

5

THE TURNING
POINT

As sure as I'm alive today I would have been a second lieutenant by Christmas, 1955, if it hadn't been for a conversation I had at Forest Hills with Renville McMann, who was the president of the West Side Tennis Club that year and a big man in the U.S.L.T.A. Mr. McMann came up to me after one of my matches in the Nationals and asked me how I would like to make a tour of Southeast Asia on a team sponsored by the State Department. I can remember exactly what I said to him. I said, "Are you kidding?" I couldn't figure out what the State Department might want with me. I wasn't exactly the ambassador type. But Mr. McMann didn't back down. He said, "I mean it. The State Department is thinking of sending a team of American tennis players on a good-will tour of Southeast Asia. And they specifically said they would like you to be on the team."

I said yes right away. I didn't even have to think about it. I told him the truth, which was that not only would I consider it a great honor to make a trip like that but I was dying for something interesting to do. He said he would let me know the details in a short time but that it looked as though Ham Richardson and Bob Perry would be going, along with me and some other girl. They hadn't decided yet who the other girl would be. I guessed right away that they weren't saying anything about the other girl until they'd had a chance to make sure that the one they picked would be friendly to the idea of going with me.

The first I knew about who had been picked was when I was in Mexico City playing in the Pan-American, and Karol Fageros saw me talking to some of the English girls at a table in the Chapultepec Club. She came over and said she was going to make the tour with me, and wasn't it great? I couldn't have been any happier. Karol is not only one of the prettiest girls I've ever met, she's also one of the nicest; I couldn't think of anybody I would rather spend a couple of months with. When Mr. McMann called me up a few days later and told me that he had asked Karol to go, and said he wanted to be sure he could still count on me, I gave up the whole idea of going into the Wac, and said, sure, I would love to go. I meant it, too. Karol and I agreed that we would have a ball together.

When we got back to the States, we made all the arrangements and wound up sitting in on a meeting with a representative of the State Department at the Vanderbilt Hotel in New York just two days before we were due to take off. All four of us were there, and the State Department man gave each of us seven hundred fifty dollars in travelers' checks, out of which we were supposed to pay for our room and board on the six-week tour. We also got all of our airplane tickets for the trip. In a way, the seven hundred fifty dollars didn't seem like any too much, but it turned out to be fine. On the flight to London we talked about how we would bunk on the trip. I remember saying something like, this doesn't seem like any too much money for such a long time, don't you all think we ought to double up in the hotels and save a few bucks? We're going to be awfully close, anyway. It seems silly not to share rooms. Karol thought it was a good idea and said so right away. Ham seemed to want a room of his own but the rest of us argued him out of it on the ground that because he's a diabetic, he, of all people, ought to have somebody with him all the time. In the end he agreed, and that's what we did.

I had a great time with Karol, who's a pale blonde and as pretty as a movie star. She was real fun. I remember one thing that happened between us when we made our first stop in Asia, at Rangoon, in Burma. I had to do my hair, and for a colored girl who has hair like mine, that's a real problem when you're away from home. I'd brought most of the things I needed--a pressing comb, a curling iron, a can of Dixie Peach Pomade hair grease, and even an old soup can with the top cut off so I could make a fire in it and heat the iron. The one thing I needed was something to put in the can to make a fire. So I went out looking for a drugstore and managed to buy some mentholated spirits which would burn in the can much like Sterno. When we got up the next morning, I got Karol out of bed to go take a swim with me in the hotel pool, and I told her that when we got back I was going to do my hair. She said that was fine because she had some letters to write.

Well, when we got back to the room, I went into the bathroom and washed my hair and dried it. Karol was sitting at the desk writing when I walked back into the room, and she took one look at me and jumped on the bed and started rolling around and laughing. I didn't blame her a bit; I was a sight. When I first wash my hair and dry it, it absolutely stands up straight. Karol had never seen anything like it before and it just panicked her. "Go ahead," I told her, "get your kicks. You'll see when I get finished."

I put some of the mentholated spirits in the can and struck a match to it and got a pretty good fire going. Then, while I held the pressing iron over the can to heat it, I put a lot of the Dixie Peach Pomade on my hair, and when everything was ready, I began to press it. Karol like to died. "What are you doing?" she hollered. So help me, I think for a while there she was actually scared. "Aren't you afraid you'll burn yourself?" she kept saying. I guess I got a little bit sensitive about it because I picked up all my stuff and went into the bathroom with it, but Karol kept getting up and peeking in to see how I was doing. And she kept laughing and laughing. She wasn't being mean, mind you, she was my friend; but she'd never seen anything like it before, and it positively fractured her. I remember I said to her, "Don't laugh at me, honey, I can't help it. Us colored girls don't have hair like yours, that's all. This is what we got to do for it." I explained to her that I didn't usually have to fool around with it myself; back home I could get it done in a beauty parlor. But, traveling like this, I didn't have any choice except to do it myself.

When I finally got through, Karol came over close to me and touched my hair and said, "Gosh, you've got really fine hair." And I said, "That's because I've pressed it. If I didn't press it with a hot iron, like this, it would be a mess." Karol couldn't believe it. "My goodness," she said, "it looks pretty."

We were getting to know each other a whole lot better. After a while I got tired of doing my own hair, and I began wishing I could find somebody to do it for me. Finally, when we got to Calcutta, I left Karol in our hotel room one afternoon and said I was going out to see if I could find a hairdresser who could do it. The first thing I saw when I got outside the hotel was a snake charmer, begging for money. As soon as he saw me he set up a shrill whistling. Then he opened up his basket so the cobras could stand up, and begged, "Alms, alms!" I must admit I was tempted to give him something, but we'd been told a hundred times not to give the beggars anything or they would never leave us alone, so I just watched the snakes for a while and then walked away. I didn't have to go far before I saw a beauty shop. I walked in and asked to speak to the proprietor. I figured I had a pretty good chance of getting what I wanted because most of the people in Calcutta are dark-skinned, and it seemed like the beauty shops ought to be used to my kind of hair.

I told him what the problem was. "My hair requires heat," I told him. "You can't do it with just a liquid. Can you take care of it for me?"

"I understand, I understand," he said right away. "We can do it for you." So I sat down and he went to work on me himself, which seemed like an encouraging sign. But after he washed my hair, he proceeded to put some liquid on it. I sat right up and protested. "What are you doing?" I said. "My hair can't be done that way." But he insisted that he knew what he was doing, and I figured the best thing for me to do was to shut up. When he started to put it up in pin curls, though, I started in again. "Lady," he said patiently, "we do the coarsest kind of hair this way. Believe me, it will work out fine." So I kept quiet and let him have his own way. But when he put me under a dryer, I really hollered. "No, no, no!" I told him. "This won't ever work!" But then when he started telling me again about how he knew exactly what he was doing, I didn't have the nerve to say anything more. I just sat back and hoped for the best. Well, you should have seen me when they combed out my hair. It was as dry as firewood; it actually crackled. After a little while, the man began to look a little worried himself, and he started combing it harder and harder. I finally stopped him. "Wait a minute," I told him, "you've got a few waves in there, anyway, don't comb them out." So I paid him the twenty-eight rupees (seven rupees to a dollar) that he said I owed him, and I headed back to the hotel. Karol came in while I was combing it out, and she just shook her head. "He sure did you up," she said sorrowfully. "The next time, you better let me do it."

The worst part of the whole thing was that we had to go to a fancy cocktail party that evening, and I'll bet we had to pose for fifty pictures. I've got a whole lot of them in my scrapbook, and until someday when I burn them all up, I'll never have a chance to forget what that Indian hairdresser did to my poor hair. I look like a Ubangi medicine man in every one of those pictures.

We had some great adventures on the tour. In Rangoon I got sick--as sick as I can ever remember being in my life. I didn't deserve any sympathy for it, though; I brought it all on myself. When we got to Rangoon we were put up with a detachment of United States Information Service girls (Ham and Bob stayed with the USIS men) because Khrushchev and Bulganin were in town on a state visit and had taken up all the hotel space. The kids were as nice as they could be to us, and one night they took us up to Mandalay for a government banquet in our honor. What a spread that was. It was the first Oriental buffet I'd ever seen, with shark's fins, lamb, veal, chicken, rice, different kinds of curries, lobster, oysters and prawns. I really stuffed myself with the prawns, which are just big shrimp; I must have eaten at least twenty-five or thirty of them. The four of us were separated, one at each table, and we all had a lot of fun trying to eat Oriental style. I did my best to copy the eating style of the Burmese, holding the bowl right up to my face and pushing the food into my mouth with chopsticks. They loved it. The only trouble was, I ate too much.

The show they put on after dinner was great, too. I really flipped over it. The dancing girls had such beauty of expression, as well as beauty of physique, that you couldn't take your eyes off them. Anyway, I noticed a couple of times that Ham and Bob were having trouble taking their eyes off them. But it was all a lot of fun, and when we got back to Rangoon the next day for another set of exhibitions, we were glad to accept an invitation to another cocktail party and buffet dinner that night. I never should have done it. We wound up in an exquisite Chinese restaurant, fifteen or sixteen of us in a handsome private room, and we ate and ate and ate. We drank a little, too, and I was feeling pretty good by the time I got to bed, early in the morning. But when I woke up I was miserable. We had twin beds, and the bathroom was around past Karol's bed. I made so many trips in there, she didn't have a chance of getting any sleep. I was doubled up with stomach pains. I tossed my cookies so many times I couldn't understand where it was all coming from. My head was soaked with sweat, and yet it was ice cold at the same time. Karol wanted to know what she could do for me and I asked her to go see if she could find some bicarbonate of soda, but there wasn't any in the hotel. I felt like shooting myself, and if I'd had a gun I might have.

After a while one of the USIS girls came up and asked if there was anything she could do. I told her I thought she'd better get a doctor, and she said she would. In the meantime, she gave me a glass of lemon water to settle my stomach, and I threw it right back up. That poor kid sat on the edge of the bed holding me in her arms like I was a baby until the doctor came. He said it was acute gastritis, and he gave me some more pills to take, but it was three or four days before I could eat a solid meal. And I had nobody to blame for it but myself.

It was a good thing Ham had a little extra money in what we called "The Captain's Fund," because all four of us got sick at one time or another on the tour, and we never would have been able to pay all those doctor bills out of our own money. The U.S.L.T.A. had appointed Ham captain of the team, and I guess the State Department people had given him the extra money to use for emergencies. Anyway, it was always a big joke with us, whenever we were spending a lot of money, that we'd probably end up digging into the captain's fund. But it was a good thing we had it when we all started getting sick. I've often thought that I hope it was the State Department's money that Ham was spending, and not his own. He's such a good guy, he never would have said.

One thing that gave us a lot of laughs was the fancy train we rode from Calcutta to Dacca, in Pakistan. In the first place, the Indian trains are the worst in the world. Nobody who has made a journey on a train in India ever would complain about the Long Island Railroad. This time, the four of us found the car to which we had been assigned, and asked the porter to show us to our quarters. None of us had paid any attention ahead of time to what it said on our tickets, and we were totally unprepared for what happened. The porter led all four of us into one large compartment and, without any discussion at all, began to show us how to make up the four beds. They all let down from the wall, two on each side of the compartment. Karol and I watched him curiously for a few minutes, and then we both interrupted him. "Hey," we asked, "where do we sleep?" The porter clearly was puzzled. I might add that he also was wholly undisturbed. Anyway, he simply motioned to the four bunks. "Here," he said, waving vaguely around the compartment. "You mean all of us?" we demanded, Karol and I staring at Ham and Bob, and Ham and Bob staring at Karol and me. The porter just shrugged; it was clear that he meant all of us, and also that he didn't much care one way or the other.

We asked enough questions to find out for sure that there wasn't another compartment available anywhere on the train. We were all going to sleep together or a couple of us were going to stand up all night in the corridor - it was up to us. Karol and I looked at each other, and we knew that, come what may, we weren't going to stand up in the corridor all night. So, figuring that somebody had to get things started, we plunked down our things on the two lowers and left the two uppers to the boys. We took turns going out into the corridor, to the one rest room, and changing into our pajamas. Ham went first, then Bob, then Karol, and then I. It was a lucky thing that Karol and I had brought along some good pajamas; we would have been crushed if we'd taken old ones. But it was fun, and it gave us something to talk about, and to make jokes about, all the rest of the time we were on tour. And even now, whenever one of us meets one of the others, the first thing we mention is the night we all slept together in one compartment on the Indian railway.

There were a lot of people standing on the streets outside the station in Dacca when we've arrived, and we soon noticed that there was something strange about the crowd. We weren't sure whether it was something that was there or something that wasn't there, but we could sense a difference. "What is it?" Ham asked me, and after a couple of minutes I finally caught on. "No women," I said, and that's what it was. In all the time we were in the city we saw only one woman on the streets. All the rest were in purdah, which means they aren't allowed to unveil themselves, or even to go out in public.

It wasn't, incidentally, that way at the tennis matches. There were quite a few women in the grandstand and none of them was veiled. Furthermore, almost all of them were, by Western standards, beautiful. I'm willing to take the word of the boys for that. Which probably means that the real motive behind the purdah restrictions is that the husbands of the Indian women don't want any other men to so much as lay eyes on them. There is nothing careless about relations between the sexes in India.

Neither Karol nor I ever went out alone with any Indian men, although from our point of view they were just as good-looking as the women appeared to Ham and Bob. Some of them had the most gorgeous, big bedroom eyes I'd ever seen. But I saw no one who attracted me specifically, and Karol and I were content to stay together whenever we went out. I'm not saying what I'll do if I go back there again.

One night all four of us were invited to a dinner party at the home of one of the richest men in Pakistan. In Pakistan you can be either extremely poor or extremely rich and this gentleman was extremely rich. He had a fine spacious house, almost entirely built of marble and every bit as cool as an air-conditioned movie in New York.

Everything was beautiful, including the plumbing, which was strictly Western style, except that it was more lavish than anything we had ever seen before. Most of the women at the party, including our host's wife and two daughters, were startlingly beautiful. with their rich brown skin, soft features, black hair and big, expressive eyes. They all wore saris, the traditional dress of the Hindu. Karol and I admired them so much that one of the daughters of the house insisted that we go into her bedroom with her and try on one. She brought out a magnificent silken sari for each of us, and with her sister's help showed us how to put it on. The sari is much like a one piece wraparound dress tucked in at certain strategic places. You achieve the proper effect by wrapping it around your waist allowing it to drape full in front, then winding it tightly around your bosom and over your left shoulder. With it you wear a white blouse, preferably with a plunging neckline. Karol and I couldn't resist going out and showing everybody how we looked, and the reaction was so good that we each took a sari home with us. It isn't good for shopping in the A&P but it's fun to wear at a small cocktail party at home. It's what you might call a conversation piece.

That was quite a party. The buffet dinner would have done the Waldorf-Astoria proud. and there was enough food for a regiment, including, of course, all the specialties of the country such as curried chicken, curried shrimp, curried rice, curried lamb, and curried heaven-knows-what. In India they curry everything, and from the visitor's point of view, it's just as well. Any time you're worried about whether or not safe to eat in a dubious restaurant or private house, you can always resolve the problem by asking for some curry. If you're worried about bugs, you can forget it nothing can survive in curry.

I was interested in the young Pakistani girls. I hadn't expected them to be quite so Western in their attitudes as I found them to be. They talked about their boy friends and their husbands just as women do at a party in the States. The one big difference is that they still have a very rigid, Old World style of courtship, except that you really can't call it courtship at all; the "engagements" are arranged by the parents when the children are quite small. But even under this system, which seems somewhat restrictive to say the least, they manage to have a pretty good time. The girls go out on dates, go to movies, play tennis, go on swimming parties, much as we do at home. The only difference is that they don't ever go out with anybody except the boy to whom they have been betrothed. Although, if you ask me, they would very much like to.

In short, they are not all that different from us. They work, they take care of their families, they worry about survival, and in general they behave much as we do except for certain national customs and except for the fact that they have so many more poor people than we have and nothing that resembles our American middle class. In Pakistan it's pretty much all or nothing, and for most of the people it's nothing.

It was an experience to remember. I've never been exactly sure why I was selected to make the tour in the first place, but I'm glad I was. I know it happened soon after the killing of Emmett Till in Mississippi, and world opinion of the racial situation in the United States was at a low ebb. So I suppose that was the main reason why I, a colored girl, was invited to help represent our country in Southeast Asia. I certainly wasn't picked because I was a champion; at the time I was champion of nothing and unlikely ever to be.

Before we left home, the State Department people had warned me that I probably would be asked a lot of questions about the Negro's life in the United States. They said it was up to me to say what I thought was right, and all they asked was that I remember that I was representing my country. I think we made the tour on a happy note, with no trouble and, for that matter, with no incidents. In a way, it was surprising that I didn't encounter more sharp questions than I did. Those who did inquire told me what they had read and said they would like me to tell them what it really was like for a Negro in the United States. I always said, well, we've got a problem, as all countries and all states and all individuals have, but it's a problem that certainly can be solved and that I firmly believe will be solved. I was always aware that some of them, especially those who had ideas of someday coming to the States themselves, would like to probe further, But I didn't see any point in going too deeply into the matter. I answered all their questions honestly, and I let them dictate how far the discussion should go.

I will say this: I was obviously the principal attraction of the group. Inasmuch as we were traveling among dark-skinned peoples, that was completely understandable. I was played up everywhere we went. Because I was a Negro, the Asians not only were particularly interested in me, they also were especially proud of me. The kids looked at me, as I played, with awe and amazement. They couldn't believe that any Negro could play tennis so well. I can testify that they loved Karol, who not only played fine tennis but also looked like a Hollywood movie star, but they unquestionably got a special kick out of me because of my color.

The tour was, I think, an unqualified success. It ended at Colombo, Ceylon, about January 12, 1956, and I headed straight for Stockholm to play in a tournament that was scheduled to begin there on January 19. Karol left Ceylon with me, on the same plane, but when we stopped at Dusseldorf, in Germany, she got off. She wanted to visit a boy friend who was stationed at an army post there, and then she planned to head back home. I got off the plane with her and stayed with her until she was met by her friends. Then I said good-bye, and we both cried. I hated to see our journey end. I'm glad to say I think Karol hated to see it end, too.

My travels, though, were far from over. I played in Cologne, in Germany, in Lyon and Gallia in France, and in Cairo and Alexandria in Egypt. I found out at least a little bit about a lot of things I never had known anything about before. Like the Pyramids, for instance. I was astounded to discover that if I wanted to explore the inner chambers of the Pyramids, I had to crawl through entranceways no more than four feet high. (And I'm five feet, ten and a half inches tall!) I also found out something about Egyptian night life, which, if you ask me, consists mostly of little rooms filled to overflowing with belly dancers. I still haven't got over how much fun it was to watch the boys watching the girls. Not that I blamed them; the way those dancers swiveled their hips was a modem engineering marvel, except that I understand there is nothing modem about it at all. They tell me it's been going on for a long, long time.

Another interesting thing that happened in Egypt was that I met a young man I liked very much. He was an athlete -- a swimmer -- and he was good to look at and pleasant to talk to, and we enjoyed each other's company. I first met him in Cairo, and I saw him for two weeks there and then for two weeks in Alexandria. He watched all my matches, brought me soft drinks afterward, and then took me out to see the sights of his Egyptian cities at night. Belly dancers and all.

The only bad thing that happened was the last night I was in Alexandria, when I thought somebody was trying to break into my room. I'd been out late, and it was about one o'clock in the morning when I was getting ready for bed. There was an enclosed porch outside my room, and just as I was fixing my hair for the night, I heard a noise out there. I stopped and listened hard, and I was sure I could hear somebody moving out there. I was scared. I picked up the telephone and hollered for the man to send somebody up, quick, right now. But he didn't understand English; apparently all the English-speaking help worked on the day shift. Oh, brother, I said to myself, ain't this a blip. I kept pleading with him desperately to send somebody up, and then I put down the phone and grabbed a tennis racket with a heavy frame on it. It made a pretty good weapon and I felt a lot better with something in my hand. Finally, somebody knocked on the door and I opened it and was relieved to see it was the night clerk. I tried to explain to him what was the matter, and I managed to coax him to open the porch door and look outside. He did, but there was nothing there. I even looked myself, and I couldn't see a thing. But I was certain somebody had been there, and I didn't sleep a wink all the rest of the night. I just lay on the bed with all my clothes on, the telephone on one side of me and the tennis racket on the other. I was ready for anything.

Perhaps it was because I had enjoyed so much being with my Egyptian friend, and perhaps it was simply that, I had been away from home too many months, but from the time I left Alexandria, I was painfully lonesome. The whole trip lasted eight months, and I really felt those last few months. Everything I did was scheduled for me; nothing was spontaneous. I hungered to be with somebody. No matter how hard I tried to think of myself as just another person, I was constantly being confronted with proof that I wasn't, that I was a special sort of person--a Negro with a certain amount of international significance. It was pleasant to think about but very hard to live with. Sure, I had a good time. I played my matches, went to parties, and talked to crowds of people; but after that there was nothing more. I thought if I only had someone of my own, someone I could completely relax with and let my hair down with, I could be happy. It was a strain, always trying to say and do the right thing, so that I wouldn't give people the wrong idea of what Negroes are like. Once these people get to know me, I thought, they will see that I'm no different from anybody else; only my skin is different. But it wasn't easy to figure out a way to get them to know me.

One thing I know for sure, though, is that I've never done anything more completely satisfying, or more rewarding, than that tour of Southeast Asia for the State Department. The experience did wonders for me, and I think Ham, Bob, Karol and I have a right to feel that we did a good job for the United States. I have a newspaper clipping in my scrapbook taken from the *New Times* of Burma, in which the writer, Kin Maung Aye, gave us an enthusiastic review despite the fact that he wasn't especially enthusiastic himself about either tennis or Americans. I like to think that he, and perhaps a lot of his readers, too, were more kindly disposed not only toward tennis but also toward Americans after we left. Here is what Mr. Aye's story said:

"I have never been much of an enthusiast for tennis, but when I was introduced to Mr. Hamilton

Richardson, U.S. tennis star, and his team by Mr. William Lipper, Public Affairs Officer of the United States Information Service here, my mind turned immediately to the exhibition matches they gave at the Railway Institute's court on their two days' visit to Mandalay. For me, the two days' exhibition matches overshadowed all others. They had everything - great tennis, thrills and all the necessary elements to rouse the spectators to the highest pitch of excitement.

"I find tennis interesting and intriguing as played by the U.S. tennis stars. They certainly are 'super' players with 'big' serves. The modern tennis, as I see it, is as different from the old as chalk is from cheese. What struck me particularly is their serve-volley game, which indeed is triumphant. Some of the people sitting beside me, watching the exhibition, queried: 'Could not the success of the big serve and volley be due to the weakness of the ground stroke?' But the American players demonstrated very clearly that they have no weaknesses. Both Bob Perry and Hamilton Richardson are giants in physique, and they packed every ounce into a colossal serve which they most ably followed into the net. Their second delivery was as powerful as their first. It carried speed, spin and accuracy. Their service was one of the greatest serves I have seen.

"A packed court crowd turned up to see Richardson play Perry. They produced a game never before seen in this country. Drives were mixed with chips and slices; no two shots were hit alike. The forehand cannot annihilate the stonewall defense from the baseline. They chopped the ball, sent it over at half pace, and even put over the crude lob of a novice-anything to throw off their opponent.

"The picture is the same among the two women players of the American team. They certainly are in the class by themselves. Miss Althea Gibson has proved that baseline tennis, when 'hotted up,' is supreme. She has many other attributes -- concentration, physical fitness, speed of foot, determination and the 'killer instinct.'

"Miss Karol Fageros, too, has everything, the big serve and net game, great ground strokes, a powerful ambidextrous drive, and a magnificent athletic physique.

"One must be frank. Messrs. Hamilton Richardson and Bob Perry, and Misses Althea Gibson and Karol Fageros really delighted the Mandalay tennis players and enthusiasts with demonstrations of their attractions."

There seems to be an unmistakable note of reluctance in Mr. Aye's "one must be frank." But that's all right. To me, it simply indicates that there was a good reason behind our tour, and if we made some new friends and lessened some hostile attitudes along the way, it was very worthwhile.

Among my most prized souvenirs of the State Department trip are two letters that came to me on stationery headed "The Foreign Service of the United States of America." One was from Becky Machemahl, one of the girls who worked for the American Embassy in Ceylon. She said, "We're still receiving glowing letters and so on about the American tennis players, and you in particular... You've no idea of the impression you made here, from the hairdresser at the Galle Face to the houseboys at our place. I'm most proud to say that you are an American... " And Bill Lipper, the Public Affairs Officer in Mandalay, wrote: "Greetings from Mandalay, where you are still the most pleasant talk of the town. The Upper Burma Lawn Tennis Association and the Commissioner both asked that I extend congratulations to you for the excellent tennis that you have been playing in India. Mandalay hasn't been the same since you left, and tennis is Topic A. I do want you to know how very much I appreciated the many things which you did in the furtherance of American traditions and objectives in our community here. It was a great pleasure to have had you with us, and I hope that you will have an opportunity to return."

So do I.

6

FAILURE, CONTINUED

If I thought -- and I have to admit I did – that winning sixteen out of eighteen tournaments from Rangoon to London on the way to Wimbledon would make me a cinch to win the tournament that tennis players always refer to as the world championship, I was mistaken. The London bookmakers made me a 2-1 favorite to win, that spring of 1956, but, understandably, they were making book on the basis of what I had done in the tournaments before Wimbledon.

They weren't thinking, for instance, of the matches I had lost to Angela Mortimer of England at Cairo and Alexandria. I thought of them, but I felt that they were merely unavoidable lapses; I preferred to think of the sixteen tournaments I had won, including the French championship at Paris, by far the most important title of any I had ever won. In that one I got back a little of my own from Angela, who had beaten me not only at Cairo and

Alexandria but in every one of the four tournaments in which we had met. I felt good about that one. I was excited, and hopeful.

As far as Paris itself was concerned, the main feeling I have about it is that if you don't know anybody there, it's just like living alone. I enjoyed being there because I'd read so much about it for so many years, about how exotic it was and how beautiful. And also because when I was in England in 1951, and Sugar Ray was touring Europe and I met him and his boys in London, all they talked about was how wonderful Paris was. They raved about it. I remembered that they had said they stayed in a hotel on the Champs-Elysees, so when I got to Paris, and was put up at the Hotel Miami just off the Etoile, I headed for the Champs-Elysees right away. I couldn't wait to see it.

It didn't strike me as such a big deal, although there is something colorful about it with the interesting shops on the avenue, the little restaurants, the night clubs and the theaters. Actually, it reminded me of 42nd Street, except that the Champs-Elysees is wider.

The most excitement I had in Paris was right on the tennis court in Roland Garros Stadium. I was playing my friend Angela Buxton in the semi-finals, and all of a sudden one of the straps on my brassiere broke. Angela came over to help me, but there wasn't much we could do about it out there in front of all those people, so I rushed off to the dressing room to repair the damage. When I got back on the court, I found myself involved in a federal case. They were having a big meeting at the umpire's chair and they told me that I'd had no right to leave the court like that without permission, and that if Angela requested it, they would default me right then and there. Angela protested that that was the last thing she wanted, so all the little men went away at last and we finished the match. I won it and went into the finals against England's other Angela, my jinx opponent, Angela Mortimer.

The final-round match was largely uneventful except for one time when I lost my temper for a second. This is what the *London Sunday Express* said about the match, which I won 6-3, 11-9:

"As always, Angela Mortimer began nervously, groping for a length, forced into wide errors by the heavy pressure, and serving double faults. She made a real fight of the fourth game but lost it after seven deuces and four advantage points. In the remaining five games of the set, she won only seven points against the American's twenty. 9-8 ?

"Though the American, at 10-9 in the second set, nervously lost her service and angrily slammed a ball far into the crowd after a double fault, she made no mistake the next time and fittingly finished a love game with an unanswerable ace down the center line."

I had become the first Negro ever to win the championship of France; in fact, the first Negro ever to win any of the world's major singles tennis championships.

That night Angela Buxton's father took Angela and me out to dinner, to celebrate. I was back at my hotel, and in bed, a little after ten.

If I were to make an excuse at all for the way I failed at Wimbledon, and I would rather not, I would have to say that maybe I was a little overtennised, after having played so many tournaments in a row. But mostly I was overeager. I wanted to win so badly that I pressed. I tried too hard. In one of the so-called warmup tournaments, at the Northern Club in Manchester, I played a genuinely tough match with Shirley Fry and beat her 6-3, 6-8, 7-5 after more than one hundred minutes of tennis that caused a writer for the *Daily Telegraph* and *Morning Post* to comment: "Two well-matched boxers fighting for the Lonsdale Belt could hardly have put more effort, physical and mental, into the contest. It was athleticism to a degree more virile than feminine... Miss Gibson, ever pressing netwards, ever on the attack, fighting every point, recoiling only to spring again, played as relentlessly as a woman ever did. Yet, if she were relentless in her determination to win, so too was Miss Fry... "

And I think Ralph Hewins, writing in the *Daily Mail*, came close to the heart of the matter when he pressed me, in a series of interviews on the eve of the big tournament, to tell him these things: "After ten years of it, I am still a poor Negress, as poor as when I was picked off the back streets of Harlem and given the chance to work myself up to stardom. I have traveled to many countries, in Europe, Asia, and Africa, in comfort. I have stayed in the best hotels and met many rich people. I am much richer in knowledge and experience. But I have no money.

"I have no apartment or even a room of my own anywhere in America. I have no clothes beyond those with which I travel around. And I like clothes. Unfortunately, I have no gift for making them, and I can't afford many of the wide variety of cheap, ready-to-wear American dresses which other American girls buy, then throw away after a few months. Mine have to do for a long time.

"I haven't been able to help my mother and my father, and the rest of my family. They are still poor, very poor. My father is a garage hand. My brother and the eldest of my three sisters go out to work. My other two sisters are at home. And my mother can't go out to work because she's too busy keeping house for the family. I am the eldest of the five children, so you can imagine how badly I feel about not helping them when I am living well and meeting all sorts of fine people."

You can see that I was feeling sorry for myself, and that's a poor state of mind for any competitor. Anyway, I was beaten in the quarter-finals by Shirley Fry. The same writer who had covered my win over Shirley at the Northern Club said this time: "Miss Fry beat Miss Gibson, 4-6, 6-3, 6-4, a reversal of the close issue they had in the Northern Club tournament at Manchester. Then I described their contest as a minor classic, not so much on stroke values as on the forthrightness of the struggle. Today, nerves, influenced by a packed Centre Court, and perhaps even by the presence in the royal box of the Duchess of Kent, played a greater part. Those of Miss Fry, who has played so many a struggle on Wimbledon's main court (this was her seventh quarter-final), were the more firm."

After she beat me, Shirley went all the way. In the final, it took her exactly fifty-two minutes to race through my doubles partner, Angela Buxton 6-3, 6-1. After trying for it for years, Shirley had finally won the championship, and it was kind and generous of her to say, as she did after it was all over, "I should not have won. Althea played so wonderfully in the last set that the pressure was on me, and I never really got a chance to play well. But she got scared. If she had crowded me at the net like I expected her to, she would have won. But she hung back, through nerves, I guess. I felt sorry for her because I know how it feels."

In the interests of total objectivity, I would like to quote from another newspaper article, this one written by Scottie Hall in the *Sunday Graphic* at the end of Wimbledon week:

"Shame on the Centre Court! Don't worry. I'm not going to bore you with a re-hash of the shameful, shabby scenes when American tennis star Vic Seixas told the Wimbledon crowd to shut up for booing him. That, too, was shame on the Centre Court. But space is short. And I don't feel like wasting it on a Yank, never mind how talented, who doesn't know how to lose. This is all about the Yank who lost with nobility. This is an attempt at a salute to Miss Althea Gibson, the colored girl from Harlem who served an ace for her race with her serenity and graciousness in unexpected, puzzling defeat. And that noise you hear is a boo from me. A boo directed at the people I hereby accuse of helping to bring about the defeat of the Gibson girl.

"I accuse the Wimbledon crowd of showing bias against Miss Gibson. I say it was this bias that helped to rob Miss Gibson of a quarter-final round victory over fellow American Shirley Fry, a victory which, early in the match, looked coolly and comfortably hers. It wasn't anything that was whispered. It wasn't anything that was shouted. It certainly hadn't anything to do with the handling of the match, which was exemplary. It was just an atmosphere, tight-lipped, cold.

"You know that wonderful feeling you get in the theatre when an audience rises to the first entrance of a well-loved star. I wish it had been like that. But it wasn't. It was an unspoken, unexpressed but felt anti-Gibson atmosphere. An atmosphere that prompted centre-court graybeards, knee-deep in memories, to talk to me later of the match's strange, 'eerie' mood. It's part of my job to smell atmosphere. Halfway through the Gibson-Fry match, I found myself sniffing hard. I didn't like the smell. This was when the gentleman from *The Times* spotted 'the strength slowly beginning to seep' from the Gibson girl. This was when I glanced along at the face of an American tennis reporter. It was tense, strained. And this was when I conveniently remembered that Yankee voice rising above the hubbub of the Press bar at lunchtime: 'So Joe Louis became a champ. And what happened? Nigger boxers came out from under every stone. Same thing if Gibson walks away from here with a tennis pot.'

"Some thirty reporters interviewed Miss Gibson after her defeat. I was one of them. She joined us, calm uncomplaining. I was as spineless as the next fellow. I couldn't forget that color, like cancer, isn't talked about. So I merely said, 'You'd like to come back next year?' And she said, 'If I'm asked.'"

Well, I meant that, all right. I had been beaten and I was disappointed, even mad at myself. But I had no intention of giving up. I was sure I had a lot of tennis left in me yet, and I wanted to get back out on that Centre Court again. I wanted another crack at those 20,000 spectators and the frightening Wimbledon tradition just as much as I wanted another crack at Shirley Fry and the rest of the girls.

I saw another example of my quite involuntary role as an instrument of international policy when I picked up a newspaper upon my return home from England and read this story:

"Althea Gibson became the unwitting center of a British hassle last week in newspaper summaries of the Wimbledon tennis championships. One paper, expressing alarm over British colonial relations in one of its sections, delivered a slap on the wrist to Britons in another. This particular edition asked the question: 'Can We Keep India With Us?' The article under the caption went on to point out that there are 650,000,000 people in the British Empire, of whom 368,000,000 are in India. It said: First, we must show by our actions that we are free from race and color prejudice of every kind. Otherwise, what possibility is there that 368,000,000 Indians will want to cooperate with us?'

"In another section of the same edition, the following is pointed out: "To pretend that Miss Gibson is just another player is to bilk the truth. She is the first colored player ever to invade a game which is riddled with snobbery, even if your skin is the same color as the majority of the other players in it. Althea wants to be regarded as just another competitor, but it was very noticeable that when her opponent at Wimbledon, that nice, natural girl, Ann Shilcock, led 5-2 in the first set, the crowd clapped for her when the players changed sides and did not applaud the Gibson girl. It is easy to say that they only applaud the player who is leading, but that doesn't happen to be true. It's easy to say that they applauded because it was an English girl leading against an American, but, that too, is not quite accurate.

"'The color bar dies hard in any sport; once it nearly needed legislation to end it in boxing in England. So when Althea, serving like a dream and volleying like a nightmare (to her opponent, that is), won the last two sets against Miss Shilcock, I could have wished that the white palms were waved a little less languidly.'"

Personally, I could have wished, as I always have in such circumstances, that I might be allowed to play tennis--win or lose--with the same purely individual responsibility assigned to everybody else. Being considered an adjunct of U.S. State Department policy, as had been the case off and on during our Southeast Asia tour, was bad enough, but having to bear the responsibility for England holding on to 368,000,000 citizens of India was definitely more than I could manage.

I was having enough trouble trying to gain control of my shots and play the best tennis I was capable of playing. Having to contend with crowds hostile to me because of my color, with newspapermen demanding twice as much of me as they did of anybody else simply because my color made me more newsworthy, and even with powerful governments seeking to use me as an instrument of national policy because of my color, seemed to me to be more than anybody should have to bear.

But I couldn't blame any of these outside pressures for my failure at Forest Hills in September. Even though Shirley had repeated her Wimbledon victory over me in the National Clay Courts Championship at Chicago, with a pretty convincing 7-5, 6-1 win, I had high hopes that I would be able to get in a good lick for my side in the Nationals. I started off well enough, going all the way through the semi-finals without losing a set. I defeated Mrs. Nell Hopman, the wife of the Australian Davis Cup team captain 6-2, 6-1 in the first round, and then I won from my good friend Karol Fageros 6-3, 6-2 in the second round. The competition got tougher in the third round but I managed to take Darlene Hard 9-7, 6-1 in the quarter-finals, and then I beat Betty Rosenquest Pratt 6-1, 10-8 in the semi-finals. That put me in against Shirley in the final. Unhappily for me, I didn't have it. Shirley's baseline game outsteadied me. I kept rushing the net, as I always do, and Shirley calmly let me play my way to error after error. She beat me 6-3, 6-4. They were the only two sets I lost in the whole tournament, but they were the ones that counted.

Even so, I felt I could take a whole lot of comfort from the way I had played, and the progress I had made, during the year. I won't pretend that I wasn't bitterly disappointed that I hadn't done better in the big ones, but I was a long way from wanting to hang up my racket. I was certain now that I was capable of playing on even terms with the best amateurs in the world and even if I hadn't been able to beat them as often as I could have wished this year, I would get them the next time around.

After Forest Hills, I accepted an invitation from Perry T. Jones, who is now the captain of the U.S. Davis Cup team, to play in the thirteenth annual Pacific Southwest Championships at the Los Angeles Tennis Club. It was my first appearance in the Pacific Southwest, and only my second visit to the city of Los Angeles. I had been there briefly in 1953 to take part in one of Ralph Edwards' "This Is Your Life" television programs, built around the life of Alice Marble. The tournament, which attracts a great many Hollywood celebrities, was a lot of fun for an old movie fan like me, especially, I suppose, because I won it by beating Nancy Chaffee Kiner 4-6, 6-2, 6-1 in the final. Nancy took me pretty good in the first set, but I broke her service in the second game of the second set, quickly built up a 3-0 lead, and after that had an easy time for the rest of the match.

I stayed in Los Angeles long enough to be the guest of honor at an exciting party at the Town Club, where Nat "King" Cole presented a beautiful 35mm camera to me as a memento of the tournament, and then I flew straight back to New York. I had a couple of weeks at home, devoted largely to a frantic effort to catch up on my mail, and then I headed for

Mexico City and the Pan-American. I beat Darlene Hard in the final of that one, and promptly headed, like a homing pigeon, back to New York. But not for long. The Australian Lawn Tennis Association had invited Shirley Fry and me to visit there and play in all their major tournaments and a few exhibitions. I was eager to go, and so was Shirley. It turned out to be a memorable trip for both of us, but especially for Shirley, as I will explain later on.

The New York office of Pan American issued me the usual envelope full of tickets, and I flew from New York to San Francisco (Shirley took off from Los Angeles) and then on to Australia with stops at Honolulu, the Fijis and Canton before landing at Sydney. We played in the four biggest Australian tournaments, the Victorian and the national championships, both at Melbourne; the New South Wales, at Sydney; and the South Australian Championship, at Adelaide. Shirley beat me in the finals of the Australian Nationals and the Victorian; I won the New South Wales and the South Australian.

I don't know why I wasn't more consistent against Shirley. When I lost, it was because I made all the errors and she played a steady, waiting game, the game for which she is famous. When I was on my game I didn't have much trouble with her, as this newspaper clipping suggests:

"With devastating power, American Negress Althea Gibson swept through Wimbledon champion Shirley Fry in straight sets 6-2, 6-4 at Royal King's Park yesterday. Shirley Fry holds the Wimbledon, U.S. and Australian titles. Althea Gibson won the French and Italian championships.

"Miss Gibson gave such a terrific exhibition of tennis that it took world champion Shirley Fry all she knew to try and cope with her. Miss Gibson has the complete game and is truly a great athlete. Her service was phenomenal as she almost invariably scored with her first serve or followed up with a high-kicking second service which was equally difficult for Miss Fry to handle. Her ground strokes matched her serve for speed and accuracy, and when the occasion demanded, a volley or a stop volley was put away for a winner with the touch of a master.

"Miss Gibson played so well despite the fact that during the warm-up before the match, a ball flew off her racket and struck her a nasty blow in the eye. After accepting first-aid treatment, she put on a pair of dark glasses and played the match throughout with them on."

We really loved the country. Australians are as easygoing and as naturally hospitable as any people in the world. And, of course, they love tennis. One of the things I remember best about our visit was the long stay we enjoyed with two doctors, Dr. Robert Mitchell and Dr. Gwonne Villiars, in their Melbourne home. Shirley and I called them Bob and Doc, respectively, and we became very attached to them. To say the very least, they treated us royally; anything we expressed the slightest wish for, they got for us. We lived a great deal better than the thirteen dollars and fifty cents daily allowance given us by the Australian L.T.A. would have permitted had we been entirely on our own.

Of course, the biggest adventure of our Australian trip was Shirley's romance. We were sitting in our hotel room in Sydney one day, soon after we had arrived from the States, when Shirley got a telephone call from an American man who introduced himself as Karl Irvin and said that she probably didn't remember him but that they had met back home. He was working in the Sydney office of the J. Walter Thompson advertising agency and he wanted to take her out to dinner. Shirley was lonesome, and eager for a change, so she accepted. But to me, she said doubtfully, after she had hung up, "I'll bet he's some old guy. I'll probably be sorry." But later that night, when she barged in from the date and found me still awake, reading in bed, she said enthusiastically, "You know, he's not old at all. He's nice."

I met Karl myself the next day and thought he was an -exceptionally nice man. There was no question that Shirley thought so; she spent every hour she could with him, and I think he proposed to her before the week was out. The night he did, Shirley and I sat up late in our room talking about it-the three of us had driven out to the beach that afternoon-and Shirley said she just wasn't sure what she ought to do about it. But she was head over heels in love, she knew that.

By the time we got to Perth, which was where our tour was supposed to end, Shirley had made up her mind. She had telephoned her parents back home in Akron and told them that she was going to stay in Australia, fly back to Sydney and be married to Karl in a month. She figured that was about how long it would take her to get ready. Karl expected to stay in Australia for a long time. Shirley knew it, but she was willing, anyway. Like I said, she was in love.

The only thing I was sorry about was that I wasn't going to be able to stay for the wedding. I would have been glad to change my plans and stick around, because Shirley and I had become very good friends, but I had made a commitment to go to Colombo, in Ceylon, to defend the championship of Asia which I had won at Calcutta the year before. So I had to say good-bye to Shirley in Perth and climb aboard a Pan-American Clipper for the flight to Ceylon, by way of Jakarta and Singapore.

Shirley, by the way, wasn't even allowed to cash in the unused return half of her round-trip airplane ticket. No matter how much she argued, pointing out that she was bound to go back to the States some time and surely was entitled to the return passage that originally had been guaranteed to her, the Australian LT.A. stuffily clung to the position that she could keep the ticket and renew it each year for as long as she wanted to, but that she couldn't turn it in for cash. Poor Shirley could have used the money for her trousseau, but there wasn't anything she could do about it. Fighting an amateur tennis association is worse than trying to fight City Hall; at least the men in City Hall are responsible to the people who elect them, but the tennis poobahs are responsible only to themselves, and they never forget it.

Traveling alone wasn't much fun after so many weeks of good companionship, but I struck up a friendship with one of the stewards on the airplane, and he took good care of me all the way to Singapore, where we had to lie over for two days to wait for a connection to Ceylon. When I mentioned to him that I was fond of playing golf, he volunteered that he had a friend, a jockey, who was a member of the Country Club in Singapore and would be glad to take us out for a round. I was delighted. I hadn't had a golf club in my hands for a long time, and anyway it would be nice to have something to do in Singapore besides just sitting in a hotel room, reading. So we made a date for the day after our arrival, and, sure enough, the steward and the jockey called for me at my hotel and took me to the Country Club for a day of golf. I got in some good shots, and of course I did my best to show off how well I could play, and the boys were vastly impressed. They said I was a natural-born golfer. I didn't bother to tell them that I'm also a natural-born basketball player, baseball player, football player, bowler, boxer, and that I shoot a pretty fair game of pool, too. I didn't want them to think I was a tomboy. Anyway, we all got along fine together, and when they suggested taking me out that night for a look at Singapore after dark, I was more than willing. I was having a good time.

The jockey's wife made it a foursome that night and we had a ball. They picked out a beautiful Chinese restaurant and I had my first true Chinese dinner, complete with chopsticks. Fortunately, I had learned the chopstick bit on my Southeast Asia tour, so I didn't disgrace myself. The food was delicious; I didn't even know the names of most of the things we ate, and I decided it was safer not to ask, but

I enjoyed every mouthful. There was a floor show, too, very lavish, very American in manner, and very undressed. And there was wine, served fiery hot in tiny little cups. All in all, it was a big night, and I would like to do Singapore again sometime when I can stay longer.

In Ceylon I won the Asian championship again by beating Pat Ward of England in the final. It was a strange sort of match. Pat isn't anywhere near as strong a player as Angela Buxton or Angela Mortimer, and I didn't have much trouble running through the first set at love. And then, I'm ashamed to admit, I started coasting, and losing. Pat had me down 5-0 before I pulled myself together, won a game on my own service by coming up with three aces, and then won four more games in a row to even it up at 5-5. After that, we each held service until the twenty-third game when I broke through. Poor Pat lost it the hard way; she served a double fault at love-forty, and that did it. I won my service easily enough, and that was that. Maybe I couldn't win Wimbledon or Forest Hills, but I sure was hell on wheels in the Far East.

There was one more appearance I had to make in Ceylon, keeping a promise I had made the year before to the girls in the USIS office. They wanted me to sing a blues program in the USIS library, and I was glad to oblige. Quite a large number of people showed up for the concert, which we put on during the noon hour, and I felt amply rewarded by their enthusiasm.

And then a somewhat travel-weary Althea got aboard another airplane, took off her shoes, stretched her long legs out into the aisle at the risk of helping the steward break his neck, and headed for New York, U.S.A. It was a long trip and I had plenty of time to reflect on what the year had brought: I was the champion of Asia and the champion of France and the champion of Italy, among other places; Shirley Fry was the champion of Wimbledon of the United States, and of Australia, and in every one of those tournaments I had been her pigeon. There was no getting away from it, Shirley had won the big ones and I had won the little ones. It had been very much her year.

All the way back to New York, between catnaps, and with the comfortingly steady roar of the four engines my ears, I thought about what I could do to make 1957 Althea Gibson's year.

7

CHAMPION OF WIMBLEDON

Now that I was an established internationalist, the U.S.L.T.A. paid my way to Wimbledon in 1957. They gave me my round-trip plane ticket and enough expense money to take care of my hotel, meals and other charges. Part of the expense money was given to me before I left, in American dollars; the rest I was to pick up from a U.S.L.T.A. official in London, and that would be in English pounds.

Sydney Llewellyn drove me to Idlewild in his car, and Buddy Walker, my old play-street supervisor and expert on saxophones, came along for the ride. Edna Mae Robinson drove out in her own car to see me off. Just as I was getting on the airplane, Edna slipped twenty dollars into my hand and told me it was for extra spending money.

I was traveling light, with just two bags, both of which I checked through. I kept my tennis rackets, one Harry C. Lee and two Slazengers, with me, because I didn't want anything to happen to them. The trip over, on a Pan-American Strato-Cruiser, was beautiful. The air was smooth and the food they served was irresistible, and I felt as though I were going away on a wonderful vacation.

Angela Buxton met me at the airport, along with a gentleman friend of hers. She was driving her little Austin convertible and, surprisingly, we all managed to squeeze into it for the ride into London. Even my two bags and my three rackets were stowed safely into the tiny trunk. Angela had invited me to stay with her in her flat in Paddington, and I was looking forward to it. We stopped for some breakfast on the way into town, then went straight to the Bat, which is in a handsome building at 97 Rossmore Court. Angela, who earns her living working for the Lily White sporting goods store (isn't that funny?) and writes for a number of British sporting magazines, has a very comfortable layout with a kitchen, bathroom, two bedrooms and a living room. She gave me a front-door key to use during my stay, saw me started with my unpacking, then hurried off to work. I had to leave that afternoon myself, for Surbiton, to play in the first of the pre-Wimbledon warmup tournaments. I was booked to play at Surbiton, Manchester, Beckenham and the Queen's Club. Fortunately, I would have to stay out of town only for Surbiton and Manchester; the others were near enough so that I would be able to stay at Angela's.

I won every singles tournament I played in, but I passed up the Queen's Club singles because I didn't want to risk going into Wimbledon all tired out. As

I told Angela, the night before my first match, I was in top shape, I wasn't tired and I wasn't worried, and if I didn't do well I would having nothing to blame it on but my lack of ability.

There must have been a lot of people in the stands the day I played my first-round match who had serious misgivings about my ability. My opponent was a Hungarian girl, Suzy Konnoczy, whose tiny size, five feet two inches, made us look like Mutt and Jeff as we walked out on the court. But Suzy was on her game that day, and she gave me a hard fight. I won both sets 6-4, 6-4 but Suzy didn't yield a point without a struggle. The way it turned out, that was the most difficult match of the tournament for me, although the British newspapers had hoped that the sixteen-year-old English girl, Christine Truman, who clobbered Shirley Bloomer in one of the early rounds, would make things hot for me when we met in the semi-finals.

I got to the dressing room about two hours before our semi-final match was scheduled, and I read all my mail, watched a few doubles matches on television, and just took it easy until they called us. Christine and I walked out together. We stopped in the waiting room just inside the center court to talk with the officials who were gathered there, and they told us the Duchess of Devonshire was in the royal box and that we should be sure to tum toward the box and curtsy as we walked out on the court. I was a little bit worried about the curtsy because I'd never tried it before, but I'd seen it done lots of times in the movies, and I was sure I could manage it. After we took care of the curtsy bit, which turned out to be not hard at all, and posed for the crowd of photographers who were lined up by the umpire's chair, Christine and I spun a racket for serve. I won and elected to serve first.

As we began to play, the crowd was very excited, applauding each good shot and humming with praise for the way Christine was playing. But after I put away the first set, and it was clear that I wasn't likely to have much trouble winning the match, everybody quieted down. It was like when the Yankees were winning at Milwaukee in the World Series. I didn't feel bad about it; I didn't blame them in the least. They haven't had a winner for a long time in England, and it was only natural for them to root as hard as they could for Christine. They were very sporting about it, though. When the match was over, and I had won, they gave me a wonderful hand. I was pretty excited. It was quite a feeling to be a Wimbledon finalist.

Before I could do anything else, I had to go to a press conference in one of the stadium offices, and after that they let me take my shower and enjoy a refreshing massage before getting dressed for the trip back to town. I had rented a small Austin to use during the tournament, and I drove in with two old friends from my A.T.A. days, Katherine Landry and Dorothy Parks, both of whom were captains in the Wac and were stationed in Germany. They had saved up their leave time so they could spend it in London and watch the tournament. I was glad they had. At a time like that, when you're building up more and more tension every day, you like to be with people of your own kind, people you can relax with and let your hair down with, and never have to be on guard with. Katherine and Dot did that for me, and it meant a lot.

That night we headed for a little French restaurant that was my favorite London eating place. It was called Le Couple, and it specialized in the tastiest filet mignon I'd ever eaten anywhere. We all had a drink before dinner. I settled for sherry-and then we tore into that steak as though we hadn't eaten for days. A waiter I'd become quite friendly with saw to it that my filet was done just as I liked it, medium rare, broiled in butter and garnished with onions. It was a delicious dinner, and when we were finished, I was ready for bed. The two captains were going out on the town, but they understood my desire to go to bed, and they went back to Angela's with me. In fact, they were my lady's maids for the night. They saw to it that I soaked in a lazy, hot bath, and then they tucked me into bed and read to me until they were sure I was sound asleep. Then they turned out the light and tiptoed out.

Right here I had to make a confession. I'd been so hopeful that I might win the tournament that, the first week I was in London, I'd gone down with Angela to her store and picked out a beautiful evening gown to wear to the Wimbledon Ball. Even worse than that, I'd worked for days on a speech to give at the Ball in case I won. I was all set. All I had to do now was beat Darlene Hard, the California girl who had won the other semi-final match.

Our final was put down for one-fifteen in the afternoon, so I got out of bed at about ten. Angela was up already, and she brought me a cup of tea in bed. After that, I got up, had my breakfast, made my bed, and got ready to go. Angela who hadn't been able to play in the tournament because she had a badly sprained wrist, was going to broadcast the matches on the television, so she had to leave early. She gave me a kiss for good luck and said she would see me after I won.

I left the flat at about a quarter after eleven and drove to the hotel where Dot and Kay were staying, and picked them up: I brought along a pretty new tennis outfit, Terrylene pleated shorts that the English designer, Teddy Tinling (who designed Gussie Moran's famous lace panties), had made for me, and a Fred Perry shirt. The lady who took care of our things in the clubhouse had cleaned my tennis shoes so that they gleamed, and as I dressed for the match. I felt that everything was just the way it should be. Everybody in the dressing room was talking excitedly about the news that the Queen was going to be there. That made me feel extra good. I would have been terribly disappointed if she hadn't been.

About an hour before the match I went out on one of the side courts to practice with Shirley Bloomer, and while we were hitting back and forth, I saw Queen Elizabeth eating lunch on the clubhouse porch. Instead of making me nervous, it made me feel more eager than ever to get out there and play. I went back into the dressing room to change into a fresh shirt, and then I was ready. Darlene and I walked out to the waiting room, collected all our final instructions, including how to curtsy to the

Queen and what to do after the match, and then we went out to play.

I won the toss again and served first. It was hot, about 96, they said, and I never felt more like playing tennis. There is something about a hot, still day that brings out the best in your shots; the sweat seems to loosen your muscles and perfect your aim. Anyway, I got off on the right foot, serving hard and well, and I won the first set 6-3 in exactly twenty-five minutes. Maybe the heat bothered Darlene more than it did me, but whatever it was, I felt all along that it was my day. When I rushed the net, I got the volley; when I stayed in backcourt, and Darlene charged the net, I passed her. I have a clipping from the *New York Times* that says: "The game grew faster as Miss Gibson's service jumped so alarmingly off the fast grass that Darlene nodded miserably as her errors mounted. It was all over in fifty minutes."

They tell me that I kept saying, "At last! At last!" All I can remember doing is running up to the net and shaking hands with Darlene and saying that she had played very well and that I had been lucky, and I was very happy. Then right away, the officials came up to us and asked us to talk over to the umpire's chair, where the trophies were spread out on a table. A crew of workmen unrolled a gleaming red carpet from the royal box to the table, and we stood at attention and waited as Queen Elizabeth followed by three attendants walked gracefully out on the court. She wore a pretty print dress, a white hat and white gloves, and she was absolutely immaculate even in all that heat. One of the officials called me to step forward and accept my award. I walked up to the Queen made a deep curtsy and shook the hand that she held out to me. "My congratulations," she said, 'it must have been terribly hot out there." I said, "Yes, your majesty, but I hope it wasn't as hot in your box. At least I was able to stir up a breeze." The Queen had a wonderful speaking voice and she looked exactly as a queen ought to look, except more beautiful than you would expect any real-life queen to look. She handed the gold salver, on which the names of all the previous Wimbledon champions were engraved, to me, and I curtsied again and backed away from her while Darlene stepped forward to receive her runner-up trophy. (I remembered that backing-away business from the movies, too.) I couldn't hear what the Queen said to Darlene, but I know Darlene was just as excited as I was. After that, the Queen turned and walked back to the royal box, the red carpet was rolled up, and the newspaper photographers began to bombard us.

While I stood there, posing this way and that to accommodate the photographers, I thought about something I had read in a book Helen Wills wrote about her career in tennis. "My feelings," she said, "when that final Wimbledon match was mine, I cannot describe. This was the prize for all the games I have ever played since I was a little girl." I knew exactly what she meant.

After all the photographs were taken, I was led inside to the television room where Dan Maskell, the professional at the All-England Club, of which

I had automatically become a lifetime member by winning the championship, interviewed me. After that I headed to the dressing room. The two captains were waiting there for me and took care of all my things while I soaked in a hot bath for a solid half hour (In the ladies' dressing room at Wimbledon, they have real bathtubs!) By the time I had dressed there was a small heap of telegrams at my locker, and I read some of them before we set out for London.

CONGRATULATIONS. EDNA CRIED WITH JOY.I KNEW YOU'D DO IT, SUGAR RAY.

THE STUDENTS, FACULTY AND PRINCIPAL OF WILLISTON HIGH SCHOOL EXTEND HEARTIEST CONGRATULATIONS ON YOUR WINNING THE SINGLES CHAMPIONSHIP AT WIMBLEDON B.T. WASHINGTON, PRINCIPAL.

CONGRATULATIONS TO A FELLOW NEW YORKER ON WINING THE WIMBLEDON CHAMPIONSHIP. WE ARE ALL VERY PROUD OF YOU. AVERELL HARRIMAN.

There were lots of others, but I barely had time to look them before I had to hurry out to the parking lot, retrieve my little Austin, and drive to Angela's. It was almost five o'clock, and the Wimbledon Ball was supposed to get under way at seven. I dropped off Dot and Kay at their hotel and raced off to get dressed. Lew Hoad, who had won the men's singles championship, and I were to be

King and Queen of the Ball. I didn't want to miss a minute of it.

Kay wouldn't go to the ball because she didn't have a formal gown. I tried to talk her into going in her uniform, on the ground that was automatically formal, but she wouldn't listen. Dot went, though, and so did Angela and her boyfriend. Dot and I took a cab from her hotel, and when we got out of it, in front of the Dorchester, where the ball was being held, a big crowd on the sidewalk broke into the most pleasant applause I had ever heard in my life. As I walked into the ballroom, everyone stood up and applauded. I was escorted to the head table and seated between the Duke of Devonshire, who was master of ceremonies, and Lew Hoad.

We had a goodly number of drinks, and then dinner, and afterward the Duke gaveled the assembly to attention and introduced first Lew, and then me. Each of us was supposed to make a speech. Mine, which I had worked on hard, went like this:

"In the words of your distinguished Mr. Churchill, this is my finest hour. This is the hour I will remember always as the crowning conclusion to a long and wonderful journey. It all started in one of New York's play streets when Buddy Walker, a play-street supervisor, reached beyond his grasp of a handful of youngsters playing paddle tennis. He said, 'Althea I believe you could become a good lawn tennis player,' and with those words he handed me my first tennis racket and started hitting against a handball court. Tonight, I thank Buddy Walker for a most satisfying victory. But the victory is not mine alone. It belongs to many people who play an important part in the picture here tonight. To mention them all would take too long, but I cannot help but recall a few whose encouragement and faith permit my presence here tonight.

"I remember particularly Dr. Robert W. Johnson and Dr. Hubert A. Eaton. It was in Dr. Eaton's home while completing high school, that I received love and encouragement. It was through Dr. Johnson's efforts and assistance that I was able to travel all over the United States and gain much needed experience.

"Also, I could not let this moment pass without special thank-you to Fred Johnson, my first coach. He was so patient with my first feeble attempts at lawn tennis. Nor can I forget my present coach, Mr. Sydney Llewellyn, whose belief, foresight and unswerving faith in my ability made me continue when I would otherwise have given up.

"I am grateful to the American Tennis Association and the United States Lawn Tennis Association for their support throughout the years.

"And how could I forget my good friend and former partner, Angela Buxton, whose friendship I shall always cherish although she always forgets to bring the cold milk in so that by the time I get up to drink it, I really have warm milk. So, Angela, please, next time let's have the milk real cold, huh?

"In addition, this victory is a profound salute to my most worthy court opponents whose outstanding ability and invincible courage and determination aroused a challenging response in me.

"And finally this victory is a sincere thank you to the many good people in England and around the world whose written and spoken expressions of encouragement faith and hope I have tried to justify, No, my friends, this victory is a thing of no small matter. It is a total victory of many nations. It is a collective victory of many champions, for each player around these tables tonight is, in his own right, a champion. True champions in a realm to which the price of admission is good sportsmanship. I am proud to have had the privilege of being a link in this world-wide chain of friendship, a chain of friendship created through the international language of tennis.

"Your Highness, my friends, I am humbly grateful and deeply aware of the responsibility involved in the wearing of this crown. God grant that I may wear it with dignity, defend it with honor, and, when my day is done, relinquish it graciously. I thank you."

After that, it was time for the dancing. Lew and I were to start it off by dancing the first dance, and he asked me to pick the song. I suggested "April Showers," and he said fine, so that's what the band played as we circled the ballroom once to get the ball started. After that everybody joined in, and the joy was unconfined. After we had been dancing for a while, Ham Richardson and Vic Seixas insisted on my singing a couple of songs. Everybody wanted me to, so I got up on the bandstand and sang, "If I Loved You" and "Around the World." I got a big hand, but, after all, under the circumstances I probably would have been applauded no matter how I sang. Actually, I was already thinking about singing professionally, so I undoubtedly took my performance a lot more seriously than the crowd of dancers did.

After the dance (I even danced with the Duke), Dot and Angela and her boyfriend and I all went to a small night club to finish off the evening. I sang a couple of more songs there, which shows you what a good time I was having, and by the time we got back to Angela's flat it was early in the morning. But it had been a wonderful evening and a wonderful day.

It seemed like a long way from 143rd Street.

Shaking hands with the Queen of England was a long way from being forced to sit in the colored section of the bus going into downtown Wilmington, North Carolina.

Dancing with the Duke of Devonshire was a long way from not being allowed to bowl in Jefferson City, Missouri, because the white customers complained about it.

And maybe best of all was the letter I got right after the tournament that said:

Dear Miss Gibson:

Many Americans, including myself, have watched with increasing admiration your sustained and successful effort to win the heights in the tennis world. Millions of your fellow citizens would, if they could, join with me in felicitations on your outstanding victory at Wimbledon.

Recognizing the odds you faced, we have applauded your courage, persistence and application. Certainly, it is not easy for anyone to stand in the center court at Wimbledon and, in the glare of world publicity and under the critical gaze of thousands of spectators, do his or her very best. You met the challenge superbly.

With best wishes,
Dwight D. Eisenhower

There is one other memento of that Wimbledon victory that I especially cherish. It's a column written by Milton Gross of the *New York Post*. Milton was with my mother and father when the news came over the radio that I had won, and he heard exactly what they said.

"I didn't think she would, my mother said. "I didn't think a Negro girl could go that high."

"I knew she would do it," my father said. "She only wanted to try for the top, and she finally made it. I knew she had the strength to do it."

"Strength?" Milton wanted to know. "What kind of strength do you mean?"

"Physical strength," Daddy said, "and any other kind of strength that's needed."

8

WELCOME HOME!

One of the high spots I am not likely ever to forget from my tennis career is my welcome home to New York a couple of days after I won at Wimbledon. I truthfully did not expect anything like what happened when I got off the airplane at Idlewild. After all, when I left for England, there hadn't been anybody there except Sydney Llewellyn, Buddy Walker and Edna Mae Robinson. This time there was a crowd, including my mother, Manhattan Borough President Hulan Jack, a city official who was called the deputy commissioner of public events and was supposed to be representing Mayor Wagner, and a whole lot of newspaper, radio and television people.

They tell me my mother was one of the first people to get to the airport, and I know she was the first person I ran up to when I got off the airplane. I guess she cried a little, and I heard her telling the reporters, "I always knew Althea could do it."

I remember thinking I was glad she did because I hadn't always been so sure. But it made me feel good right down to the tips of my toes to see Mom so happy. And a few hours later, when we got to 143rd Street, I saw that Daddy was taking it big, too, with all the people on the block standing on the sidewalk and him leaning out of the third-floor window and waving and hollering at me. It was a large day. There had been a big breakfast celebration at the home of Bertram L. Baker, the executive secretary of the A.T.A. before the ride up to 143rd Street, and then there was all that excitement up there. It was hard not to think about other days on the same street, days when I felt as though I were carrying home a precious trophy if I had under my jacket a mushmelon that I'd snitched at the Terminal Market. Some man standing on the sidewalk asked me, as I started into the apartment house, if I had any message for all the kids on the block. I sure had. "Stick to paddle tennis," I told them, and I wasn't fooling.

I was truly moved by the expressions on the faces of the people on the street. I won't ever forget being congratulated by Queen Elizabeth, but I am telling the plain truth when I say that it meant a lot to me to have all those people come out of their tired old apartment houses up and down 143rd Street to tell me how glad they were that one of the neighbors' children had gone out into the world and done something big.

The next day, the second day I was home, was another exciting one. The City of New York threw one of its traditional ticker-tape parades for me, from the Battery all the way up Broadway to City

Hall, where Mayor Wagner was standing on the front steps waiting to give me the medallion of the city. A little later he gave it to me all over again at a wonderful luncheon at the Waldorf-Astoria, which people like Sarah Palfrey Danzig and Bobby Riggs and Vincent Richards came to, and which was a very special page for my memory book. I still have in one of my scrapbooks, the beautifully engraved menu from that luncheon. There was cold vichyssoise, roast salt meadow lamb, "The Vegetables of the Garden," pineapple dessert surprise, mignardises (which are like petits fours), and demi-tasse. It was some fun, and it was printed right on the menu that it was a luncheon given in honor of Miss Althea Gibson by the Honorable Robert F. Wagner, Mayor of the City of New York. I felt very proud.

Of course, as is always the case with an athlete who has just won something important, it wasn't long before I had to push all the Wimbledon glory and excitement into the back of my mind and start worrying about how I was going to do at Forest Hills. First, I went out to Chicago for the National Clay Courts tournament, which I won. Then I set to work getting ready for the big one.

I must admit I took time out to read some of the newspaper clippings Angela was good enough to send me from England, and one in particular, an editorial that appeared in the *Evening Standard*, made a lasting impression on me. It said, in part:

"More than the Negro people should benefit from Miss Gibson's victory at a delicate period of racial emphasis in world affairs. It further underlines the willingness of the British to take to their hearts those of any race, creed or colour. And it shows that somewhere in the great American dream there is a place for black as well as white, in this instance for a courageous and conscientious Harlem urchin."

That was nice to read, even the slightly scary part about the importance of my victory "at a delicate period of racial emphasis in world affairs." I couldn't help but wonder, my God, what am I supposed to be, a special assistant to the Secretary of State, or something? But I made up my mind I wasn't going to dwell on what had happened already. I wanted with all my heart to become the champion of the United States, and that was the next order of business.

First, though, I had the pleasure of playing for the U.S. in the Wightman Cup matches against Great Britain. This is the closest an American girl can come to Davis Cup competition--- at least it's international, country against country-and I was happy to be picked for the team. I would be less than honest if I didn't admit that I had been hotly resentful about not being picked in 1956. I played good tennis all that year and wound up ranked No. 2 in the United States. But the people who picked the Wightman Cup team were careful to go strictly by the 1955 rankings, not by what we were doing in 1956, and because I was ranked No. 8 in '55, they were able to justify passing me up. There is no doubt in my mind that they meant to pass me up and that they were just looking for an excuse. I didn't like it. But all my bitterness was forgotten when I put on the white blazer that is given to every member of the Wightman Cup team and went out on the Edgeworth

Club courts at Sewickley, Pennsylvania in August, 1957 to play for the United States. Somehow it was a lot more exciting than just playing for Althea Gibson. For the first time I could really understand what the boys meant when they said that playing in the Davis Cup matches is different than playing in any other tournament, that it gives you a funny feeling to hear the umpire call out, "Advantage, United States," instead of "Advantage, Mr. Smith." It was quite an experience, and I was especially happy that I played well enough to help our United States team win for the twenty-first consecutive time since England last won in 1930.

Sarah Palfrey and Margaret duPont like to tease me about the day I first put on that Wightman Cup blazer. I'm such a big girl that it's very understandable, but my blazer was much too short in the sleeves. I didn't want to say anything about it because I hated to seem bigheaded, or make a nuisance of myself, but the girls tell me that we were all sitting around Captain Margaret's room waiting to go out on the courts when I got up and turned slowly and worriedly in front of the mirror, trying to get a good look at myself. "I'd rather not seem like I'm too fussy," I said finally, "but don't you think these sleeves are too short? After all, this is the first one of these I ever bad, and I want it to be right." Everybody laughed, but they all agreed with me that they were much too short and offered suggestions about what ought to be done about it, and I really felt as though I belonged. I went right out and beat Shirley Bloomer of England 6-4, 4-6, 6-2 in the first match of the series. In my second match, I beat Christine Truman, the bobby-soxer I'd played at Wimbledon. It was a good warmup for the big one at Forest Hills.

I stayed at the Vanderbilt Hotel on lower Park Avenue during the week of the Nationals. The Vanderbilt is famous as a tennis hotel, and a lot of the players were staying there. They even supplied a car to take us out to the stadium every day.

On the courts, everything went well for me. Of all people, I drew Karol Fageros as a first-round opponent. It was the second year in a row that I put Karol out of the tournament, and I was especially unhappy about being the cause of her going out in the very first round. As a matter of fact, she almost put me out. She played beautifully, and each set was a real battle before I won, each time by the same score 6-4. I wanted badly to win, of course, but as I told Karol after the match, I had mixed emotions about it. It wasn't fair to the customers, anyway, putting out the best-looking girl in the tournament so early. I'm sure the men in the stands could have shot me.

After Karol, I had a comparatively easy time making my way through the draw to the finals. That first-round match was far and away my most difficult. I won from Elizabeth Lester, Sheila Armstrong, Mary Hawton and Dorothy Head Knode without losing a set. A sports magazine said I played as though I were serenely aware that I was the star. I don't know about that, but I do know I put everything I had into it. I was confident that I would win but I was also worried that I might slip into overconfidence and blow my big chance. I didn't slip.

It seemed almost fitting that the girl who fought her way through the other half of the draw to meet me in the final was Louise Brough, the former champion of the United States and three-time champion of Wimbledon, the same Louise Brough whom I had played in that first important Forest Hills match of mine, seven years before.

On the day of the finals, I got up early and set about making my preparations. Sydney Llewellyn, who would be sitting with all the dignitaries in the West Side Tennis Club marquee to see me try for the title, had arranged for Pat Hicks, a hairdresser friend of his in Harlem, to fix my hair in the morning. It was Sunday, but she opened her shop especially for me. It was on 125th Street, I just off Seventh Avenue, and I drove there alone. The coach met me there, and after I had my hair done, I decided to leave my car parked on 125th Street and I drove back to the Vanderbilt with him in his car. We had breakfast at the hotel with Tommy Giangrande, the vice-president of the Harry C. Lee sporting goods company, for which I work. (It's a typical amateur tennis player's job; I get seventy-five dollars a month for helping to promote their products and for serving on their advisory board.) We had a long, lazy breakfast and then all three of us drove out to Forest Hills together. It was quite different from my first trip out there, when Rhoda Smith and I had taken the D train and then the F train and then had walked to the stadium. For that matter, everything was different. I was a finalist. Win or lose, I was going to play for the women's singles championship of the United States. I was already the No. 2 ranking woman player in the country, and if I could just win this one match, nothing under God's blue sky could keep me from being ranked No. 1 next year. That was really something. I was excited. I was confident, too. I don't mean that I wasn't nervous, because I was. But I was nervous and confident at the same time, nervous about going out there in front of all those people, with so much at stake, and confident that I was going to go out there and win.

I won fairly easily. Louise just didn't seem to have it my more. She tried hard, and she played fairly well in spots, but she no longer was the player who had outlasted me in that storm-postponed match way back in 1950. She had done well to play her way into the final. I beat her 6-3, 6-2, and the *New York Herald Tribune* said the next day, "there never was any doubt of the result." I didn't very often try to hit the ball as hard as I can because I felt that it was smarter to let Louise make the errors, and that's pretty much the way it went.

It was a marvelous feeling to see that last point go home and know that I had done it. I took a quick look at Sydney in the marquee, and he was grinning like a little boy. I wondered if the folks were watching on the television set back on 143rd Street. I shook hands with Louise, posed for a couple of dozen photographers, walked up in front of the marquee to accept my trophy from Vice President Richard Nixon, and talked endlessly to reporters before I went in to take my shower. The most popular question seemed to be whether or not this victory was as exciting as winning at Wimbledon. I told them the simple truth. Winning at Wimbledon was wonderful, and it meant a lot to me. But there is nothing quite like winning the championship of your own country. That's what counts the most with anybody.

I don't think anything that has ever happened to me could match the feeling I got when I stood next to the Vice-President and made a little speech about how appreciative and humble and grateful I was for all the good fortune that had come my way, and then, as I stood there with my head bowed, still dripping wet with sweat from the hot match, I heard the volleys of applause beat down from the tiers of seats all around the beautiful old stadium. The newspapers said the next day that the oldest officials couldn't remember such warm, sustained applause. All I know is that nothing quite like it had ever happened to me before, and probably never will again.

Sydney and I, along with a young protege of his, Billy Davis, had dinner with Tom Giangrande at Frank's Restaurant on 125th Street. That's the elite restaurant of Harlem, and I guess it must be one of the few restaurants in the world where almost all the customers are colored and all the waiters are white. That, Frank says, is because he thinks there ought to be at least one place where a colored man can have his meals served to him by a white man. I don't know how important that is, but I know the food is good there. We had a real celebration, the four of us, and then we went back to the Vanderbilt and put on a little party for my family and friends. By the time I got to bed I'd really had it for the day. But what a wonderful day it had been.

9

WHAT NOW?

All of my problems weren't, of course, solved because was the champion tennis player of the world. Not by a long shot. I was only thirty years old and I had the best part of my life still to live. I had to think about making enough money to support myself, about fitting myself, a Negro girl, into the larger world that I had come to know and to enjoy, and about whether or not I wanted to get married-and if I did, what was I going to do about it? As far as making money was concerned, I had my mind pretty well made up. I might play professional tennis if a good opportunity presented itself, but I wouldn't become a professional unless I thought I saw a chance to make a lot of money. I didn't want to be a teaching pro all my life; I would rather remain an amateur, earn my living doing something else, and play tennis strictly for kicks. Furthermore, I knew what that something else would be. It would be singing. I was very serious about it and I was, and am, sure of my ability to make the grade as a singer of popular songs.

Way back when I used to play hooky to hear the singers at the Apollo, I always had the ambition to be a singer myself when I grew up. I used to buy all the latest song sheets, learn the words by heart, then stand in front of a mirror for hours, practicing, expressions and all. It wasn't hard at all for me to imagine that I was the new Ella Fitzgerald. Once, I think it was in 1943, I even got up the nerve to enter an amateur show at the Apollo. I was dead serious about it; I even got my gang there as a sort of claque, to make sure I got my share of the applause. I won second prize and was supposed to get a week's engagement singing in the Apollo stage show, but the manager must have forgotten all about it because all I got was a ten dollar bill that he gave me on the show that night. But I couldn't complain. That ten dollars bought a mess of fried chicken, collard greens and root beer.

The saxophone that Sugar Ray bought me, and the band work I did while I was going to high school in Wilmington, sidetracked my singing interests for a while, but saxophone or no saxophone, I used to grab every chance I got to sing on stage in both high school and college. I wanted to take music as a minor subject in college, but my faculty advisers talked me out of it. They said that being an athlete and a musician wouldn't mix. I think they were wrong. It's funny, because later on, after I won at Wimbledon and Forest Hills, I had the same argument with Sydney Llewellyn. Maybe I'm just stubborn but I don't see any reason why I can't play tennis and work at being a singer, too. The one doesn't necessarily have to take away from the other.

For that matter, Sydney always has, in a friendly way, given me a hard time about my singing. I remember once we were at a party at the home of a friend of ours, Frieda Harris, on West 159th Street in Harlem, and Sydney told me I couldn't sing my way out of a paper bag. "We've got a fellow right here at the party who can beat you singing," he said. He meant Bill Davis. Well, I couldn't let a challenge like that go unanswered, so I agreed to sing a couple of songs, and have Bill sing a couple, and then let the guests at the party vote in which of us was the better singer. Bill won the vote, and Sydney didn't let me forget it for a long time.

It was my English friend Angela Buxton who helped me make my first serious singing effort. She knew how much I liked to sing and how serious I was about it, and in 1956 she arranged for me to make some test recordings in London. One of her friends, Jerry Wayne, an English recording star, took charge of the session as a persona favor to Angela. Angela instigated the whole thing. Jerry not only set up and supervised the making of the records he even introduced me to Al Jackson, who is the oversea publicity representative for a lot of American musical performers, including Louis Armstrong and Duke Ellington. Everybody was as nice to me as they could be. But nothing ever happened with those records. I played them for all my friends when I got back home, but that was all. There was no crowd of agents, band leaders or A&R men knocking down my door trying to sign me to a contract. Any time I went to a tennis party, I was always asked to sing, and I always got a big hand, but that was still amateur night at the Apollo.

When I finally managed to convince Sydney that working toward a singing career wouldn't necessarily wreck my tennis game, he made arrangements for me to study with Professor James Kennedy, who is the director of speech and voice at Long Island University. Professor Kennedy gave me a lot of speech tests on tape, and then, in the late fall of 1957 and the spring of 1958, I began working with him three times a week in his office at the university. He was very encouraging, and helpful, and I began to feel that I might really have a chance of getting somewhere. Then, to make things twice as exciting as they ever had been before, Abbe Niles, who is a member of the West Side Tennis Club, called to tell me that he was on the committee organizing a testimonial dinner at the Waldorf-Astoria for the Father of the Blues, W.C. Handy, the wonderful old man who had written "Memphis Blues," "Beale Street Blues," "St. Louis Blues" and so many other great songs. Abbe wanted to know if I would come to the dinner, and especially if I would sing a few songs as part of the program. I said I would be happy to, that I would be proud to be there. With Professor Kennedy as my voice coach, I think I got by all right. I sang an obscure production number that Mr. Handy wrote way back in the twenties - it didn't even have a title - and I think he got a kick out of it. I know I did. I'll always remember standing on the dais in the grand ballroom of the Waldorf that night, singing that great man's music to him while he sat there, blind and weak and old but still cheerful and still interested and still very much with the beat, listening intently and applauding softly when I finished. Mr. Handy only lived a couple of months after that night. I like to think that he had a good time at his dinner.

As so often happens when you are doing something with an unselfish motive, and glad to do it, I got a good break for myself the night of the Handy dinner. Among the people I met was Henry Onorati, the vice-president of Dot Records, who invited me to make some test records with an eye toward recording a long-playing album of popular ballads. I did, and we did. The album was released in May, 1958, and my professional singing career was officially launched when Ed Sullivan asked me to sing on his Sunday night television program the same week. Of course, I couldn't be sure whether the Sullivan invitation came because I was a good singer or a good tennis player. But either way, I've been getting a chance to learn something about singing, and I couldn't ask for anything more. I figure it's much the same as it is in tennis; you have to be a little bit lucky to get your big chance, but once you get it, you're entirely on your own and you had better put everything you've got into it.

Me being that kind of never-say-die competitor, I couldn't resist saying to Sydney, who was standing in the wings waiting for me as I came offstage after singing that night on the Sullivan show, "What was that you said about me not being able to sing my way out of a paper bag?"

Actually, I have no burning desire to set the world on fire as a singer or, for that matter, as anything else. I feel that I've established myself as a person, that I've made a place for myself in the world, and I'm happy. I don't feel I'm missing out on anything. All the good things, I'm sure, will come in time. Even a man. I admit I think a lot about getting married. Of course, having spent almost all of my grown-up life concentrating on playing tennis, with very little time left over for socializing, I'm no authority on the boy-girl bit. For instance, the only reaction I had the one time I was proposed to was puzzlement. The man said to me that he thought it would be a good idea for us to get married, and even though he seemed to be in dead earnest about it, I just couldn't take it that way. He didn't give me a ring or do anything except simply suggest that we get married, and I couldn't help but think, isn't something supposed to happen? Anyway, one thing I'm sure of is that I'm not going to throw away whatever chance I have of doing something with the success I've been able to achieve. I'm not about to throw away everything for love. I can do without a man if I have to. I've done it for fifteen years and I guess I can do it for a while longer.

I don't feel I'm missing out on anything, really. All the good things will come, like I said, even though it may take a little time. For that matter, you can enjoy yourself being single; you don't have to tie yourself down. Sure, it can be lonesome sometimes, but it has its compensations. You can work out the kind of schedule that suits you best, without worrying how it might affect somebody else, and you can make the most of the pleasures that are most meaningful to you - like, in my case, playing tennis, singing, listening to records, watching television, going to the movies, and seeing my family and friends. The people who came up with you and struggled with you are the ones you turn to when you need somebody. Take it from me, when you have a friend you have a gold mine.

As far as the color question is concerned, I have no feeling of exclusion anymore. At least, I don't feel I'm being excluded from anything that matters. Maybe I can't stay overnight at a good hotel in Columbia, South Carolina, or play a tennis match against a white opponent in the sovereign state of Louisiana, which has a law against such a social outrage, but I can get along without sleeping at the Wade Hampton and I don't care if I never set foot in Louisiana. There is, I have found out, a whole lot of world outside Louisiana - and that goes for South Carolina, Mississippi, Georgia, Alabama, and all the other places where they haven't got the message yet. Actually, I think there has been a lot of good will be shown on both sides lately, and I think we're making progress.

I am not a racially conscious person. I don't want to be. I see myself as just an individual. I can't help or change my color in any way, so why should I make a big deal out of it? I don't like to exploit it or make it the big thing. I'm a tennis player, not a Negro tennis player. I have never set myself up as a champion of the Negro race. Someone once wrote that the difference between me and Jackie Robinson is that he thrived on his role as a Negro battling for equality whereas I shy away from it. That man read me correctly. I shy away from it because it would be dishonest of me to pretend to a feeling I don't possess. There doesn't seem to be much question that Jackie always saw his baseball success as a step forward for the Negro people, and he aggressively fought to make his ability pay off in social advances as well as fat paychecks. I'm not insensitive to the great value to our people of what Jackie did. If he hadn't paved the way, I probably never would have got my chance. But I have to do it my way. I try not to flaunt my success as a Negro success. It's all right for others to make a fuss over my role as a trail blazer, and, of course, I realize its importance to others as well as to myself, but I can't do it.

It's important, I think, to point out in this connection that there are those among my people who don't agree with my reasoning. A lot of those who disagree with me are members of the Negro press, and they beat my brains out regularly. I have always enjoyed a good press among the regular American newspapers and magazines, but I am uncomfortably close to being Public Enemy No. 1 to some sections of the Negro press. I have, they have said, an unbecoming attitude; they say I'm bigheaded, uppity, ungrateful, and a few other uncomplimentary things. I don't think any white writer ever has said anything like that about me, but quite a few Negro writers have, and I think the down-deep reason for it is that they resent my refusal to turn my tennis achievements into a rousing crusade for racial equality, brass band, seventy-six trombones, and all. I won't do it. I feel strongly that

I can do more good my way than I could by militant crusading. I want my success to speak for itself as an advertisement for my race.

For one thing, I modestly hope that the way I have conducted myself in tennis has met with sufficient approval and good will to assure that the way will not close behind me. I feel sure that that will be the case: this isn't, I'm convinced, a one-shot proposition. Any other Negro man or woman with the ability to compete on the national tournament level will get a fair chance. The U.S.L.T.A. works closely with the A.T.A. in examining the qualifications of Negro players, and, in effect, any player strongly recommended by the A.T.A. for a place in the national championship draw is accepted without question. The A.T.A., of course, is careful not to recommend any but fine players, which is as it should be. Eventually, I hope, our players will be able to earn their places in the draw the same way the white players do, by competing in all the recognized tournaments that lead up to the national championships. Meanwhile, it is heart-warming to me to see as many as half a dozen Negro men playing at Forest Hills, as was the case in 1957. Their presence there, I feel, is the best answer I could possibly make to the people who criticize me for failing to do as much as they think I might do to help my people move forward.

Trying to be objective about it, I suppose some reporters might feel that I'm a cold sort of person. Even my friend Angela Buxton once wrote in a magazine article that when she first met me she thought me "cold, unapproachable, assertive and domineering." And Sydney Llewellyn, the person closest to me of anybody outside my family, once told a reporter, "The only trouble with Althea is that she doesn't mind hurting people." With this kind of testimony staring me in the face, I have to concede that I don't always charm everybody I meet. The reason, I think, without being psycho-analytical about it, goes back to my childhood. I grew up a loner, suspicious, withdrawn, slow to like people, wary about trusting any part of myself to anyone else. It isn't easy to change your personality. I still keep to myself and I know I hold back until I'm as sure as I can be that it's safe to let down the barrier. I'm not a cold person, underneath; but I'm afraid sometimes I appear to be. It just goes to show you that you shouldn't judge a book by its cover. First impressions aren't always true ones.

These days, my life consists mostly of a series of tournament tours, involving pretty much the same routine no matter where I go. Between trips -- each trip usually includes a number of tournaments -- I may have anywhere from a week to a month at home, during which I try desperately to catch up on all my other responsibilities, from answering mail and visiting my family to taking singing lessons and going on furniture-hunting expeditions. The tournaments not only are the amateur tennis player's way of working at his trade (I know I shouldn't call it that because we don't make any money out of it), but they also provide us with one of our greatest rewards, the opportunity to see the world, meet a lot of interesting and often famous people, and enjoy a style of living to which most of us distinctly were not accustomed before we got into tennis. Take, for instance, my South American-Caribbean trip in March, 1958.

When I got back from my second visit to Los Angeles for the Pacific Southwest tournament, in the fall of 1957, began to think about making a South American tour. It was a part of the world I had never seen, and I was sure it would be an exciting trip. Eddie Herr, who runs the Good Neighbor tournament in Miami every year, sent me a list of the scheduled South American and Caribbean tournaments, and I picked out five that I would like to enter. That's the best part about being an internationally ranked amateur tennis player; it's the next best thing to having a travel agency send you a whole bunch of colorful brochures and invite you to pick whatever trips you would like to make, free. The tournaments I selected were in Barranquilla, Colombia; Caracas, Venezuela; San Juan, Puerto Rico; Montego Bay, Jamaica; and, finally, on my way back home, the Good Neighbor.

All five tournaments promptly informed me that they would be glad to have me, and they all chipped in to pay for my round-trip airplane ticket. They sent the money to the Pan-American office in Miami, which mailed the tickets to me in New York.

Sydney drove me to Idlewild on the morning of March 1, and I flew from New York to Montego Bay, changed planes there, and flew on to Barranquilla. It's a beautiful city, and I had a fine week there. The tournament started the day I arrived, but I had drawn a first-round bye and didn't have to play my first match until the next day. It was so hot that none of the matches began before two o'clock in the afternoon, when the breeze cooled things off somewhat, and they usually kept playing right into the evening, finishing up under lights if necessary. As a matter of fact, my first match was played entirely under the lights, and I liked it very much. It was cool, the lighting was excellent, and the ball wasn't at all hard to follow.

Except for the time you spend on the court, you don't wear yourself out when you go to these tournaments. We were mostly content to live the good life sleeping late in the morning, with a late breakfast taking a swim in the hotel pool, sunbathing for a while, then going to the club for lunch and the matches. We almost always stayed at the club for dinner, and then by the time we got back to the hotel it was time to go to bed, unless you were lucky enough to have a date. At Barranquilla, as at almost every tennis tournament, there was one gala social function during the week, a reception and dance for the players, club officials, and local big shots. Other than that, things were very quiet.

I should add that the tournament was less placid than the social life--for me, anyway. Young Janet Hopps of Seattle, Washington put me out in the semi-finals of the singles 3-6, 6-3, 7-5 after I had built up a 5-3 lead in the second set and needed only one game to close out the match. I had a little better luck in the doubles; I played with my old traveling companion Karol Fageros and we beat Maria Bueno of Brazil and Lois Felix, a Connecticut girl, in the final.

From Barranquilla I flew to Caracas, with stops on the way at Ciudad Trujillo and Maracaibo. I had much more fun there, as far as the tennis was concerned. I won the singles by beating Maria Bueno in the final, and Karol and I won the doubles again, this time from Maria and Janet Hopps. I really had to work for that singles win, though. Anybody who thinks tennis players just coast on these wintertime tours should have seen me sweating out that match. Maria, the Brazilian girl they call "The Little Saber," was very much on her game, and she gave the big crowd, which quite naturally was rooting hard for her (inasmuch as she was not only the underdog but also a South American and therefore one of their own), all the excitement they had hoped for. I won the first set easily enough at 6-1, but then, in the second set, I fell behind, 5-4, with my own service coming up. Serving is one of my strong points, but this time I served badly. I suppose the ecstatic shrieks of the crowd on every point Maria won might have made me press too hard. Whatever it was, Marla put away the first two points of that tenth game for outright winner, and finally, at 15-40, I committed the unpardonable sin of double-faulting on set point. That evened the match and we went off the court for a ten-minute rest period. Winning that second set had steamed up Maria's fighting spirit, and she kept the pressure on me all the way through the third set before I finally broke her service at 7-all and went on to win 9-7. I felt that I bad really earned that one.

The highlight of the trip was an excursion set up by the tournament committee to a magnificent resort hotel located some four thousand feet above the city, which itself is three thousand feet above sea level. It's accessible only by cable cars, which go right up the side of the perilously steep mountains. We were all a little skeptical when we were put in the car, which holds twelve or fourteen people; you feel as though you're just suspended in space, and you can't help wondering if the cable is going to bold up. But we made it safely, and we really enjoyed the visit. The hotel had a skating rink, swimming pool, observation tower, and all sorts of handsome dining and entertainment rooms. We were amazed when they told us that there were only seven couples registered in the whole hotel that day. Maybe it's a little too remote, and undoubtedly a lot too expensive, to attract larger numbers of people.

One thing that happened to me on this part of the tour served to convince me that I hadn't lost my old touch when it came to relations with the opposite sex. There was this Venezuelan tennis player whom I had noticed playing doubles a couple of times, and there was something about him that I instinctively liked. Also, I was lonely. You can get very lonesome when you're traveling around like that, especially when there is nobody in the company to whom you feel close. So I made it my business to speak to him; I even invited him to have a drink with me. And while we were sitting there, talking about tennis and about places we had been and people we knew, I blurted it right out that I liked him every much. I must say he took it calmly. In fact, he took a sip from his drink and looked at me kind of speculatively across the top of his glass and said, well, that was very interesting and certainly very flattering to him, and he would drink hard on it and let me know. He didn't say what he would let me know, and I didn't ask. But I was already wishing I hadn't broken my firm rule against having anything to do in a romantic way with another tennis player. I've seen so much careless swapping of partners among the tennis crowd that I've always sworn that was one trap I would never fall into. I'd rather kill an afternoon in the movies any time. But here I had gone and done it--well, I hadn't really done anything, but I had left myself wide open to this fellow and I was as vulnerable as hell. I regretted it.

I regretted it a whole lot more the next day when he came up to me and said that he had thought about what I had said and he was sorry but he didn't think he was going to be in a position to do anything about it. For crying out loud, all I'd done was tell him I liked him. I felt like a fool. I suppose only another woman can know and appreciate just how much of a fool I felt. I don't think I'll ever do anything like that, again.

Our next stop was San Juan, where I stayed at the Caribe Hilton and loved every minute of it. That was really it. In the first place, it's an ideal spot for a tennis tournament because the hotel, tennis courts, swimming pool, and beach are all located right on the same grounds, and what more could anybody ask for? As I told the people there, I would like to be invited back every year; they'll never have to coax me, that's for sure.

The only thing I was sorry about was that I didn't play better in the final, which I lost to Beverly

Baker Fleitz, the pretty California girl with the two forehands. Beverly is ambidextrous, and good. I started out by staying in the backcourt against her, figuring that I would let her come to the net and then pass her. But Bev got away to a quick 3-0 lead and I changed my mind in hurry and reverted to my usual pattern of following my service in to the net and looking for the kill shot. Unluckily for me, that didn't work any better, and in the end I wound up playing mostly defensive tennis, which is emphatically not my cup of tea, and losing 6-4, 10-8. I never like to lose but I was especially unhappy about this one because Bill Harris, the chairman of the tournament committee, and Welby Van Horn, the Caribe Hilton professional, had done so much for all of us players that I wanted to put on the very best show I could for them. I'm sure the gallery enjoyed the match, however. They gave Bev a noisy band when she put away the last point. And all I could do was tell myself ruefully that you can't win them all.

One of the unusual things about the Caribe Hilton tournament is that the tennis players, who are popularly supposed to be terrifically tight with their own money and free only with other people's, got together and threw a cocktail party for Harris and Van Horn and the other members of the committee, just to show their appreciation for the wonderful time they had had. I don't think I ever heard of that being done before, but I think it was a fine idea.

Incidentally, although I was the only Negro guest at the Caribe Hilton during the time of my stay, I couldn't possibly have been treated more cordially or with more consideration. Along with the other players, I was allotted cabana space on the ultra-exclusive Caribe Hilton beach, and I couldn't have lived it up any more if I had been a millionaire in my own right. A millionaire with a white skin, at that.

Speaking of money, I ought to spell out the way an amateur tennis player deals with the financial problem on tour. As I said, the airplane tickets, calling for first-class passage and including meals, were mailed to me at home. Then, as I checked in at each tournament, I was given a cash expense allowance, conforming with international regulations, to pay for my hotel room, laundry and cleaning, tips (which are a major item for traveling tennis players, including, as they must, service personnel at both the hotel and the tennis club), and other incidentals. We can sign for our meals, but if we want a drink or a package of cigarettes we have to pay cash. We have to pay cash for taxicabs and telephone calls and a lot of other small items that have an unpleasant habit of adding up. There has been, in the last year, agitation to reduce the daily expense allowance for a touring player, and I believe the figure of eleven dollars and twenty cents was mentioned as a sensible sum. There I wouldn't be anything sensible about it at all. How would you like to be trying to live in a strange city, putting up at a fairly decent hotel, and paying all the different charges I've mentioned, on eleven dollars and twenty cents a day? There aren't many cities left on the tennis circuit, in any country, where the cheapest room in any respectable hotel can be had for less than seven or eight dollars a day, and more often than not you've got to pay ten or twelve dollars and like it. If you were operating on eleven dollars a day you would be in the red before you even got started.

Some people persist in the scandalous belief that tennis players clean up financially. The only ones, to my knowledge, who do are the ones who play on Jack Kramer's professional tour, or perhaps a few amateurs who are blessed with extraordinary talents for manipulating dice or cards or for judging the comparative speed of race horses. It would take a true financial genius to make a stake on a tennis player's expense account.

The expensive living I enjoy on the tournament circuit disappears in a hurry when I get back home. I can't afford it. I do have a nice place of my own now, in an apartment building on Central Park West -- the back of the building faces Harlem and the front overlook the beautiful green grass and wide open spaces of Central Park, which I think is a nice touch -- but I don't have much furniture in it yet and I have to be real chinchy about things like food, entertaining, and recreation. I save a little money, but very little, from my expense allowances and the seventy-five dollars a month I earn from my job as a consultant to the Harry C. Lee sporting goods company. My singing has now begun to bring in a little money, and what with one thing and another I manage to get by. But I'm an expert at making a dollar stretch.

My tennis trophies and other trophies like the Didrikson Zaharias Trophy which I won for being picked as the Woman Athlete of the Year for 1957, take up a lot of space in the apartment and make up in a way for the scarcity of furniture, but most of them are still in boxes. I don't dare take them all out because if I did I wouldn't have time to do anything but polish them. I've got enough cups and plaques and statuettes to fill a corner of a warehouse, and I've also got some handsome and useful things like tea sets, butter dishes, cake plates, cocktail shakers, chafing dishes, serving trays, and what not. I'm guaranteed lifetime customer for the silver-polish industry. Come to think of it, I'll also have to keep a little gold polish on hand. My Wimbledon trophies are beautiful gold silvers, and I am very proud of them and I intend to keep them shining.

Of course, I hope to add some more trophies to my collection before I am through, maybe some more amateur ones and maybe some professional ones, too.

That's one thing about the life of a tennis champion; you never can rest on your victories, unless you retire, and I'm not ready to retire yet. With Sydney working along with me, I will keep going right back into training as each new season approaches, just as I did when I got back from the Caribbean and began promptly to prepare for the 1958 Wimbledon and United States championships. I knew I wasn't going beat anybody with my reputation or my newspaper clippings; I would have to beat them all on the tennis court. If I ever showed signs of forgetting that, Sydney was right there to remind me.

Sydney is not only a fine teacher of tennis, including both strokes and tactics, he is also something of a psychologist. He keeps after me all the time. First, he pounded to make me think and act and play with the idea in mind that I had what it takes to become the champion. And after I made it, instead of letting up, he pressed me all the more. "You've got to hit that ball with all your strength and attack forcefully, and overpower your opponent. You've got to hit with pace and with depth, and put that championship power and determination pride behind every shot. Never let up, and don't every change from the championship way of hitting. You were hitting the daylights out of the ball last year. You were hitting it with force. You've got to hat it even more forcefully, you've got to hit it with daring. You're the champ, you can take chances, you can hit all out on every shot. You've got the ability and you've got the experience and you've got the control and the power. All you have to do is use it. Stand up there and swing freely and hit with force. Absolutely defy the ball to go anywhere except where you want it to go. That ball isn't going to talk back to you. You're its master.

It is, you see, Sydney's idea that I should fill my mind with positive thoughts and give no house room at all to negative thoughts, to doubts or fears. "You're going to win" is the only attitude he will countenance. "You're going to hit with force, as forcefully as you can, and never let up and you're going to hit the ball long, with the kind of depth that keeps your opponent back on her heels on the defensive, just like in a prize fight, then you're going to open up the court with a forcing shot and then your power is going to take advantage of that opening and put the ball away, and you're going to still be the champion because you're going to play like a champion."

He psychologizes me, there's no doubt about it. But I like it. It keeps me on my toes. It reminds me that I can't coast, that I mustn't take anything for granted, that I can't give away any games or even points, that I must play power tennis all the time because that's my game and that's what made me the champion.

The subconscious mind acts as a private tape recorder, Sydney says, and then, in a time of crisis, when you're out there all alone on the court and the championship is going to be won or lost in a few swift exchanges of shots, you play these thoughts back to yourself and they mean something to you and you respond to them and they become part of the attacking force you muster and they help you beat back your challenger because that's the way a champion does. If you have negative thoughts on your private tape recorder, those are the ones that come through at the time of crisis, and they defeat you.

Sydney has something there. He cites, as an example the night I left Forest Hills back in 1950 leading Louise Brough 7-6 in that celebrated third set. Rhoda Smith took me home with her and patted me on the back all the way, and in her apartment that night she wouldn't let anybody talk to me about the match. "Even if you lose. tomorrow, honey," she told me "it won't make a particle of difference.

You did yourself proud already." She meant well, of course. She wanted to ease my mind and relax me and turn away the tension. But Sydney says she did exactly the wrong thing, and I believe he's right. Somebody, Sydney says, should have been talking to me like this: "You were hitting a great tennis ball out there today. You were hitting the ball with pace, and you were hitting it long. You showed Brough more raw power than she's ever seen come off a woman's racket. You had her on the run. You're going to beat her tomorrow you're going to finish her off, because you're going to go right out there and do it again. You've got nothing to lose and she's got everything to lose, and you're going to walk out there and tee off with all your strength and power, and she's going to have to play it safe and hope she gets it back and hope you miss and make errors. But you won't. You'll hit the way you hit today, and you'll win, and you'll be on your way to the championship."

I forced myself to keep those words of Sydney's in my mind every minute when I went back to London for the 1958 Wimbledon tournament. Winning that one meant a whole lot to me. Not only would the championship be an important asset to me whether I became a professional tennis player or a singer, or both, but there was a question of pride involved too. In sports, you simply aren't considered a real champion until you have defended your title successfully. Winning it once can be a fluke; winning it twice proves that you are the best. I was passionately determined that there wasn't going to be any "one-shot" tarnish on my Wimbledon championship.

They made me the favorite to win the tournament but there certainly were plenty of people who weren't sure that I would -- partly, I think, because I hadn't looked too good losing some matches on my Caribbean tour and partly because I lost to Christie Truman in one of my two singles matches in the Wightman Cup play that preceded Wimbledon. But I knew what they didn't know, that I had experimented with my game in some of those matches, trying to find out what I could do as a back-court player, letting the other girl take over the net, where I usually station myself throughout most of the match. Because I'm strictly an attacking player, serving hard and running to the net and putting away the volley, I didn't do very well in the back court. But I did sharpen my ground strokes and improve my passing shots, and I think the experience did me more good than harm, although I was miserable about our losing the Wightman Cup to the English girls, 3-2.

When Sydney and I had our last talks before I flew to England, there was no doubt in our minds that l would stick religiously to my tried and true serve-and-run-to-the-net tactics at Wimbledon. That's what I did, and the results were all that we had hoped they would be. I had only one hard match in the whole tournament, against Shirley Bloomer, the No. 1 ranked British player, in the quarter-finals. Shirley won the second set after I had won the first, and she had me down 2-0 in the third set before I got the grease going in the frying pan and ran off six games in a row for the match, 6-3, 6-8, 6-2.

The set Shirley took from me was the only one I lost in the whole tournament. I beat Ann Haydon 6--2, 6--0 in a semi-final match that took only thirty-one minutes to play, and then I won from Angela Mortimer 8-6, 6-2 in the final. It was a wonderful feeling to know that I was not only still the champion, but, even more important, was clearly the champion, even in the minds of those who had chosen to doubt me after my first victory at Wimbledon in 1957. I felt that I bad answered the big question.

Eleven foot faults were called against me in the first set with Angela and at one point Angela had me down 5-3 and at set point. But I managed to pull it out with a few hard service aces, and things went much better in the second set. I didn't want any bad feeling between us. I won, and that was all that mattered. The Duchess of Kent did the presentation honors from the Royal Box this time, and I danced at the Wimbledon Ball with another Australian, Ashley Cooper, who had succeeded Lew Hoad as the men's singles champion. I didn't know if I would ever dance at another Wimbledon Ball, so I stayed up late and enjoyed this one to the fullest. It was nice to be the champion; I'm not ashamed to admit I liked it.

Between tournaments now I go to see my family and friends like the Robinsons and the Darbens, and I still spend a lot of time in the movies. There would be no hard times in Hollywood if there were more people like me around. I would like to find out about the legitimate theater but that's one of the things that will have to wait until I have a steady income. I've been exposed to it once. Sarah Palfrey took Sydney and me to dinner at Sardi's and then to see Lena Home in Jamaica. It's the only stage play I've ever seen.

I keep busy around the apartment. For one thing, I'm pretty mechanically minded and I get a kick out of putting in plugs and fixing broken fixtures and things like that. If there's anything around the house that needs fixing, I always try it myself before I call up somebody else to do it. I've always been that way. Once, when I was living with the Darbens, Mom Darben mentioned that it didn't look as though her sons would ever get around to fixing the lights in the house. One of the ceiling fixtures had to be replaced and three or four of the table and floor lamps weren't working. I told her not to worry, I'd fix them for her, but when I started to work on them, she only got more worried. She kept shaking her head doubtfully. "Well," she said, "it'll either be fixed or we'll all be burned up." When I got finished and went down into the cellar and turned the juice back on, and all the lights went on like they were supposed to, I was a hero.

You can see that my pleasures and interests are simple. I have no lofty, overpowering ambition. All I want is to be able to play tennis, sing, sleep peacefully, have three square meals a day, a regular income, and no worries. I don't feel any need to be a King Midas with a whole string of people hanging on me to be supported. I don't want to be put on a pedestal. I just want to be reasonably successful and live a normal life with all the conveniences to make it so. I think I've already got the main thing I've always wanted, which is to be somebody, to have identity. I'm Althea Gibson, the tennis champion. I hope it makes me happy.

The End

AFTERWORD

DON FELDER

As a young boy growing up in New York, my siblings and I knew about Althea because my mother would keep us informed of what Althea was doing at all times. I remember seeing Althea at the ticker tape parade on July 11, 1957. Althea's mom, our aunt Annie would always keep my mom, her niece informed of Althea's activities. Our household knew when Althea was on What's My Line, Ed Sullivan and traveling abroad.

When Althea wrote her Autobiography, "I Always Wanted To be Somebody," my daily prayer included, "Lord let me be somebody"..

When my mom asked Aunt Annie, whom we called Aunt Belle and asked if Althea can come to our school, JHS 73 on McDougal Street in Brooklyn, Althea rose to the occasion and arrived at the school wearing her white Wightman Cup jacket. This was in 1961. Today when I speak to classmates from JHS 73, they remind me of the day that Althea Gibson came to our school. To this day, I am remembered by my former classmates as Althea Gibson's cousin.

Years before Althea passed away, Aunt Belle called me and said 'You're in New Jersey and live near Althea. Please call her at this number and try to get in to assist her. After many unanswered calls and voice messages I left, I gave up. While attending an event in New York City, I saw Mayor David Dinkins and told him of my unsuccessful attempts to reach Althea and that I had given up. Mayor Dinkins told me to don't quit, continue calling her and bug her. I called again and left messages to no avail.

On September 28, 2003 I learned of Althea's death while watching the news. It was reported and many still believe that Althea had no family. Althea Gibson has family in nearly every state within the United States. Althea and the late Claude Brown, author of *Manchild In the Promised Land* were first cousins. Our ancestry is from Clarendon County in South Carolina where nearly everyone is related or connected in some way. Althea is also related to the show business family, the Wayans.

Before the funeral service, the Newark Museum in Newark, New Jersey held a wake in the museum for family and friends and colleagues of Althea. There I met Althea's longtime friend and caregiver Frances Clayton Gray, whom I became friends with and assisted with the Althea Gibson Foundation after the funeral for several years. Also at the wake was a doctor friend of mine who when he saw me and my mother asked why we were there. I informed my doctor friend that Althea and my mom were first cousins and asked why he was there. I learned from my friend that he was Althea's orthopedic doctor. He and I never had reason to discuss her when we were together.

Through Fran Clayton Gray I obtained much of Althea's personal items and learned much about Althea's life so much so, I felt that I was intruding in her life. What I learned was that I have traveled in many of the same countries as Althea did. Also, when assisting Fran Gray in packing Althea's clothing and small trophies for a display at the unveiling of the Althea Gibson stamp at the South Carolina State Museum, to my surprise I saw the uniform from the 1984 Olympic Games in Los Angeles. I too own that Olympic uniform as I was one of the team runners who delivered the flame to the 1984 Olympic Coliseum prior to Rafer Johnson running up to light the stadium cauldron to start the Games of XXlll Olympiad.

Althea was there during the time that I was. I've found photos of Althea in Jamaica and Curacao. I was in meetings at the same building that Althea was in Jamaica and operated a business in Curacao where Althea gave speeches and met with the ministry of culture and sports. I've traveled and worked in many Asia and European countries that Althea played in and visited.

Althea was an amazing woman and far ahead of her time. She enjoyed her life of travel and the many people whom she called friends. Her dear friend Fran told me that Althea would have loved me. I truly have grown to love and admire Althea as I continue to learn more about her life. She loved her family and they loved her. Althea was truly a special Somebody.